DEFEAT TO DESTINY

DEFEAT TO DESTINY

FROM SETBACKS TO SUCCESS

TONY MACK II

Performance Publishing
McKinney, TX

Photographs and images are provided by the author and/or used under permission or license where applicable. Some images may be enhanced or generated using artificial intelligence.

ISBN:
978-1-961781-83-2 (hardcover)
978-1-961781-92-4 (ebook)

Library of Congress Control Number: 2025908979

ADVANCE PRAISE FOR *DEFEAT TO DESTINY*

"Every day we wake up with a new challenge or an idea how we can accomplish greatness, it's always come down to the fact of how hard you are willing to work and T Mack embraces those challenges and pushes you further than you ever thought was imaginable!"

— MICAH PARSONS
NFL ALL-PRO LINEBACKER, DALLAS COWBOYS

"There's an art and science to teaching; they call it pedagogy. I knew T Mack possessed it as a trainer because boxing is a very grueling sport that many quit after the first or second day, but T Mack has a way of making you want to come back."

— AMARI COOPER,
FIVE-TIME PRO BOWL WIDE RECEIVER & ENTREPRENEUR

"In order to trust the process, one has to believe in its trainer. That belief starts or doesn't start the moment one walks through those doors. T Mack right away brings the best out of you and has a special way to keep you leveling up day by day. That is what he did for me and continues to do with everyone he comes in contact with."

— BRANDIN COOKS
12-YEAR NFL VETERAN | HUSBAND | FATHER | ENTREPRENEUR

TABLE OF CONTENTS

FOREWORD

by Cam F. Awesome

Fuck Tony Mack.

I know. You are already thinking this is the strangest way anyone has ever started a foreword. Well, I'm not anyone. I have always marched to my own beat: I didn't have a boxing coach or trainer. I let random people in the audience work my corner on fight nights, and I was even kicked off the Olympic boxing team. I have an odd sense of humor.

Everyone thinks *Rocky* is the greatest boxing movie ever, but it's based on a flawed concept. Getting punched in the head a lot does not lead you to a championship; it gets you CTE. A fight, like business, is a game of wit. It requires endurance, resilience, risk-taking, adjusting when and where needed, and sometimes holding on for dear life until you can get your feet under you again. Tony Mack is a fighter of that caliber.

If you're still waiting for me to say my opening statement was a joke, it's not. That's truly how I felt about Tony before we ever met. I already had hundreds of fights under my belt, but everywhere I went, people just kept talking about this up-and-coming fighter named Tony Mack. Anytime someone would bring him up, I would say, "Fuck Tony Mack," and it became a bit of a running joke.

A few years later, I found myself crashing on Tony's couch whenever I was in the Dallas area for a training camp, and I didn't want to pay for a hotel room. From the minute I first met Tony in person, I realized I couldn't dislike him, whether I wanted to or not. This is a man who has the smile of a politician and the punch of a super heavyweight. Tony tries harder than any human being I have ever met. Whatever he does, he gives 100%. That's why I know this book will be a powerful tool for its readers.

There was a point where I knew Tony looked up to me. Hell, he had me write the foreword to this book, so he might still be in some ways. But I can honestly say that I now look to Tony as a mentor in life and business because of all he has accomplished. I am an author, a motivational speaker, traveling the country for events, a winner of more USA Boxing fights in my weight class than any other fighter, and I have a Netflix documentary. But Tony still pushes me to want to do better every day. He has an amazing ability to authentically and genuinely engage with people in ways I have never seen before.

I know that, if he were able to do it, I can do it too. Tony did not start boxing because he was special. He was anything but special. But you don't have to be special to become special. The work he put into transitioning from a fighter to a successful business owner is truly admirable, and I am thankful Tony gave me the honor of writing this. If I could bottle the essence of what makes Tony Mack the success he has become, I would never need to motivate anyone.

If you picked up this book to get ahead in whatever your passion in life is, then you came to the right place. If Tony Mack can do it, you can too.

Cam F. Awesome

AUTHOR'S NOTE

This is my story as I remember it. Some details, names, timelines, and identifying information have been changed to respect the privacy of people in my life. A few conversations are reconstructed from memory to reflect what I believed, felt, and learned in those moments. I'm not here to expose anyone. I'm here to tell the truth of what shaped me, and to share the lessons that might help you in your own fight.

PREFACE

"What you're about to read is my truth."

Not everyone will agree with how I tell my story, and that's okay. I'm not here to glorify my past or point fingers. I'm here to be real. I wrote these words because I believe in telling the truth as I lived it, and because I believe God put it all in front of me for a reason.

Every setback. Every missed opportunity. Every open door I almost didn't walk through. Looking back, I see it wasn't just grit or hustle that carried me through; it was divine timing. God was working even when I didn't realize it, and he's still working now.

If you had told me when I was a kid growing up with a single father in the rougher parts of Dallas that I would one day become a professional boxer, coach elite fighters, train NFL players and celebrities, and succeed as an entrepreneur, I would have thought you were crazy. The odds said I should have failed. Many people I grew up with didn't make it out. I had every chance to get pulled into the wrong things or end up in a place I didn't want to be.

But what I remember most isn't the negatives; it's the people who believed in me and the lessons that kept me moving forward. My Pops wasn't perfect, but he was a driving force. He instilled respect, discipline, and a strong work ethic. My aunts stepped in with love and stability. My grandmother was the rock of our family. Their support gave me the belief that I could do anything, even when school failures made me think otherwise.

I didn't start boxing until I was twenty. Within a few years, I became a six-time Dallas Golden Gloves Champion, a Texas State Champion, and a member of the USA Boxing National Team. I turned pro and went 13-1-1, winning the Texas Super Middleweight title. People tell me, "Boxers train their whole lives and never get that far." I know. But perfection was never my goal; it was to become the best version of myself.

A detached retina ended my career early. I could have given up. Instead, it launched me into my true calling as a trainer, promoter, and entrepreneur. I've achieved more outside the ring than I ever could have inside it. That's why I wrote this book, because I know there's more for you, too.

This book isn't just a memoir. It's a manual. Every chapter holds a lesson that becomes a discipline, earned through struggle, failure, and faith. Boxing taught me that scared money doesn't make money; you can't win by only playing defense. Business taught me the same. Both require preparation, setbacks, title shots, and the constant fight to defend what you've built.

And both taught me that none of it matters without purpose. The Bible says we can gain everything we desire and still be left with nothing if it doesn't align with what God created us for. Everything I've achieved was by His grace. Grace doesn't mean the hard parts are skipped. It means the timing is never random, and the work is never wasted.

This is my story, but it's meant to unlock yours.

INTRODUCTION

I believe with everything in me that nothing in life happens by accident. Every struggle, every delay, every detour serves a purpose. Even this book, especially this book.

What you're holding has already lived one life. I released this book once before, then pulled it back. Not because the story wasn't true, but because I wasn't done becoming the version of myself who could stand behind these pages without flinching. So here it is again: rebuilt and reborn. Stronger. Clearer. Louder. This is the version that's meant to last.

I wrote this with one goal: to leave you stronger than you were before you opened it.

My story isn't about perfection. It's about persistence. It's about refusing to quit when the odds are stacked against you. It's about taking lessons from the boxing ring, family struggles, bad decisions, and hard seasons, and turning all of that into fuel that can help somebody else keep going.

Before we get started, here's how this book works.

If you take nothing else from these pages, take this: your setbacks can become your setup. Your story, just like mine, can change lives if you're bold enough to own it.

Part I is everything before the gloves, the foundation, the faith, and the early lessons that shaped me long before anyone called me a fighter.

Part II takes you into the ring, round by round, through the moments that tested me, humbled me, and taught me what discipline really looks like.

Part III is different. It's built like a mental training camp, with rounds for reflection, rounds breaking down the books that shaped me, rounds looking back at the moments I wish I understood sooner, and rounds studying life the way fighters watch tape. These aren't punches. These are perspectives.

Throughout the book, you'll see Corner Questions and short Reflection breaks, plus a Discussion Guide in the back. Think of them as your corner team—places to pause, breathe, and apply the lesson before stepping back into the ring. Use them however you want: to journal, to talk through with someone you trust, or simply to sit with. While this book is a story, it's also a guide. And this is just the beginning. As you read, don't just look for my journey. Look for your own.

PART I
BEFORE THE BELL

"The fight starts long before the bell ever rings."

Before I ever threw a punch in the ring, life had already taught me how to take one. These rounds aren't about titles or belts, they're about surviving, learning how to stand tall, and trusting that every scar is training for something bigger.

My early years—before boxing gave things direction.

DON'T LET YOUR ENVIRONMENT DEFINE YOU

"You don't choose the fight. The fight chooses you."

Every fighter's journey begins long before stepping into the ring, rooted in faith, discipline, and love learned in the middle of adversity. To truly understand my path, you have to start with my Pops' story, which ultimately starts with his mom, my grandmother.

You see, my grandmother is an angel on earth. This powerful woman raised eleven children during a time when women didn't have the rights or respect they deserved. I've never seen her smoke, drink, or cuss. She's buried four of her own children, from car accidents, cancer, and murder, and even some grandchildren and great-grandchildren. Yet through it all, she kept praising God. Her steady spirit set the tone for our whole family, and her prayers carry a power you can actually feel in your chest when she would speak in tongues. She's ninety-six now and still the anchor holding us all together.

My Pops grew up in Robbins, Illinois, just outside Chicago, one of the toughest areas around back then. The irony is, Robbins wasn't always like that. My grandparents had moved there from Arkansas to give their kids a better future. My grandmother's mission was always to keep the family together, which wasn't easy given that my grandfather worked as a Chicago police officer in the '60s while they owned a restaurant together. That stability didn't come easy, and I grew up hearing how hard they fought to keep us grounded.

By the early 1980s, Pops hit a crossroads. Sometimes change is planned, and sometimes life forces your hand. For him, it was the latter. A year before I was born, he got caught in the middle of a shooting and took a shotgun blast that sprayed buckshot all through his body. He survived, but it shook him to his core. He realized how fast things could go bad if he stayed where he was. Around that time, his first cousin had moved to Dallas and kept telling him about new opportunities down south. Between the close call and that push from his cousin, Pops packed up, brought a few of my aunts and uncles along with him, and started over in Texas.

In 1984, my Pops met my mother in Dallas. Nine months later, I came into the world. We hear all the time, especially in the Black community, about single mothers raising kids alone. My story was the opposite. My mom left, and my Pops raised me by himself.

My mom was born in Fort Worth and grew up in Dallas. She became a young mother long before she met Pops, still a kid raising kids. She met Pops when she was 18, and that's when I was born. They tried to make it work, but they were both young and still figuring life out. They split when I was five. After they separated, she drifted in and out of my life. She struggled with support growing up, and some of those patterns repeated in her own early years as a parent. I didn't understand any of that as a kid; I just felt the absence.

I didn't come from money. I came from meaning.

Before anything else, Aunt San was the aunt who, outside of my father, raised me the most. She believed in me from the start and was my first steady example of love and routine, long before I understood what those things meant. She moved to Dallas with Pops and was the one who really taught me structure, faith, and how to pray. Everything from how to carry myself to how to talk to God, she poured into me first. Her influence shaped me well before those Chicago trips ever did. Being around her made life feel predictable in a way I really needed. Most of what I learned early on came from watching her before I ever learned it from anyone else.

Not long after, Pops found out her two older daughters had been staying with my maternal grandfather. One day, he showed up at his door with them, tired of babysitting. Pops took them in like they were his own. That's the man he was. He didn't have to, but he did.

Pops raised me to survive first, fight later.

Pops made another big move when I was about six. When I was born, my mom gave me her last name, Taylor. For the first six years of my life, I was Anthony Taylor.

I don't remember any paperwork. I just remember waking up one day and my name feeling different. Later, I learned Pops had pushed hard for it—he wanted me to be Tony Mack II, to carry his name and what he believed it meant. Somehow, he got my mom to sign the papers.

As a kid, it didn't feel like a legal change. It felt like a claim. Like Pops was telling the world, this one is mine. And whether my mom ever fully forgave him or not... that's how he made sure my identity wore his stamp. I remember one Christmas when my mom got me a Dallas Cowboys jacket, but it was green and orange instead of blue and silver. That didn't stop me from wearing it every day. People joked it was bootleg, and it probably was. But to me, it didn't matter. What mattered was that she tried. Those gestures were rare, so every time she showed up, I held onto them. Part of me kept hoping each small effort meant things might change.

Those early experiences shaped me more than I realized. I was always looking for approval, always needed to know I did things right. If I put on my shirt by myself at two years old, I'd ask, "Did I do it right?" When we played sports, I needed someone to tell me I was good enough. When kids made fun of me, I laughed along to keep from feeling hurt. I didn't have the words for it then, but I chased reassurance the way some kids chased excitement.

In 1989, Pops bought his first house in Pleasant Grove to give us a better life and get away from the streets. Back then, it was an all-White neighborhood, and we were the minority. For a while, it felt peaceful. We had an older White neighbor who was kind as could be; he'd let me pick pecans from his tree and sit on his swing talking for hours. His wife had passed, and he treated us like family. Those quiet moments made the world feel simple in a way that didn't last long.

But neighborhoods change fast. By the early '90s, "White flight" had turned Pleasant Grove into what some people now call the Dirty Grove, a place that's been featured on *The First 48*. Pops hates it when I say that, but it's the truth. The energy around us got heavier, and you could feel it even as a kid.

God was building my foundation long before I knew I'd need it.

Even so, Pops kept hustling. I can't remember him ever having a regular nine-to-five. He was entrepreneurial, owned a restaurant and a janitorial-supply company, sold cassette tapes and men's and women's clothing, whatever it took. Our bills were always paid. When he couldn't be around, my aunts filled in. It was like having both worlds, a strong father figure and loving women who kept me grounded.

That's around when I met Big Kev. He was about five years older, the neighborhood clown who could tease you without making you feel bad. I'd walk past his house, and he'd always have a joke ready. One day, I saw him under my Pops' car, helping fix it. Pops saw what I saw: a good kid with a big heart, and took him under his wing, like he had so many others. Big Kev became like the big brother I never had, an older-brother type of influence who made the block feel safer. Having someone older look out for me gave me a confidence I didn't always feel on my own.

Pops wanted to show the young men around us that they didn't need to sell drugs or rob people to make money. He gave them real work, selling cassette tapes, doing chores, fixing cars. That was his way of keeping them out of trouble. When Pops was gone, Big Kev would look after me. We became tight, and I got close to his whole family. His older brother had been murdered a few years before, so Pops being that mentor figure mattered even more. I didn't grasp the weight of what Kev had lost, but I knew Pops filled a gap he really needed.

Pops was like Furious Styles from *Boyz n the Hood*, tough, conscious, always dropping knowledge. He'd load twenty young Black men into his janitorial van and take us to see Minister Louis Farrakhan speak. Whatever people think about Farrakhan, he pushed education and empowerment in the Black community, and Pops wanted us to hear that. I didn't catch every message back then, but I could feel how much Pops wanted us to think bigger. He showed me that a man could be strong and soft at the same time, firm when needed, but compassionate too. He taught me how to shake hands, make eye contact, be respectful, and earn respect before expecting it. Those small lessons stuck with me before I even understood why they mattered. By age 10, I was already learning how to hustle. Pops put me and my friends on corners selling cassette tapes, incense, clothing, whatever legal thing he was moving that day. Being trusted with responsibility that young made me feel like I had a place in his world.

Every story has a starting point, and mine began before I ever laced up gloves.

From the time I was little, Pops made sure we stayed connected to our roots. Throughout my childhood, even after we settled in Pleasant Grove, he'd drive or fly me to Chicago often to visit family. I loved those trips, the big gatherings, the cousins piled into the living room, the energy of a house that never felt quiet. Our family was so large it felt like a tribe; everyone was like brothers and sisters. Walking into that house always made me feel like I belonged to something bigger. But being the kid from Dallas, I never quite fit in at first. Up there, my cousins thought I was too happy-go-lucky, and they teased me for it. In Dallas, I fought kids on the block; in Chicago, I found myself trying to prove I belonged in a different way. It was confusing trying to match both worlds, but I learned fast how to adjust. Those moments shaped me, not because of who they were, but because of who they pushed me to become.

That's also where I learned what family really meant. I never had a relationship with my mom, so I had no connection to her side of the family. But my Pops' side, they stuck together, even when they teased me for being different. Their teasing never pushed me away; it somehow made me feel included. What I do remember most about those trips is being made to go to church every single time. I didn't always want to go, but I never questioned why they brought me. Didn't matter if I was in Chicago or Dallas, somebody was taking me to service. And it wasn't just Sunday mornings; there were revivals, midweek services, and Sunday school at my grandmother's church, the Church of God in Christ, a whole different level of strict. The rules felt heavy sometimes, but the routine kept me steady.

All of it, the structure, the discipline, the faith, became part of me. I'm grateful for both my parents' influence, even if they came at it from different angles. My Pops and Grandma shaped my core, and my Aunt San gave me the day-to-day foundation I needed. Everything I am started there: in that house, in that hood, in that family. Pops showed me how to move like a man. Grandma showed me how to pray like one. Aunt San showed me how to live like one. Together, they gave me everything I needed to face whatever came next. Those lessons became automatic long before I realized how much they'd matter. The fight didn't start in the ring, it started the day I learned who was in my corner.

REFLECTIONS

IT COULD ALWAYS BE WORSE

> *No matter how rough life gets, someone's got it harder.*
> *Gratitude and adaptability turn struggle into strength.*

To understand why I don't hold my circumstances against my parents or use them as an excuse for what I didn't achieve, you first have to realize it could have been worse. That's something I carry with me in everything I do. Sure, things can always be better, but if you're drowning in self-pity, convinced no one has it harder than you, I guarantee there's someone out there who would trade places with you in a heartbeat.

Nothing in life stays the same forever. What's working for you today might shift tomorrow, sometimes before you even notice. My family taught me that you have to adapt, not complain. That's one thing I'm proud to say I learned early on: they never stayed stuck.

THE PATERNAL IMPACT

> *Respect is power.*
> *A firm handshake and integrity mean more than any title.*

Pops taught me that, as a man, your word is your bond. You don't want to be known as untrustworthy, especially in the hood, and my Pops always had that mentality. He told me to shake a man's hand and say "yes, sir" or "no, sir" when asked a question, always looking him in the eye.

To this day, my Pops will still act like he's gonna swing on me if I don't show people the same respect he taught me. I'm a grown man, a professional fighter who's been punched by some of the strongest in my weight class, and I'm still afraid of my Pops because of how deeply he instilled the value of respecting my elders. That lesson shaped everything about the way I carry myself.

A REAL FATHER

> *Fatherhood is leadership in motion. Strength and consistency shape a child more than words ever could.*

For a young boy growing up, there are certain things only a father figure can teach you about becoming a man. Some may take that the wrong way but hear me out before jumping to conclusions. Now that I'm married and thinking about fatherhood myself, I have nothing but respect for women, as people, as parents, and as partners. But of all the things I have to be thankful for in life, my Pops is first and foremost. If not for him, I would never have had a real family, including all the amazing women who helped shape who I am.

THE RIGHT ONES STICK AROUND

> *People come and go, but divine timing leaves you with the ones meant to stay.*

People come and go in life. It doesn't matter who you are or what you do; some relationships strengthen, some fade, and some fall apart completely. Over the years, I've had all three. Some I miss, some I barely noticed slipping away, and some I still cherish. What's consistent in every case is that the right people stay through the hard rounds, even when you don't realize you're fighting.

GOD'S TIMING

> *Everything that happens sets you up for something bigger and better.*

Looking back, I can see how every piece of my childhood was preparation. The struggles, the moves, the people who stayed and the ones who left. None of it was random. God was positioning me for something I couldn't see yet.

Pops, Grandma, Aunt San, even the hard parts of Pleasant Grove, it all built something in me. God was laying my foundation long before I knew I'd need it.

CORNER QUESTIONS

1. What's one major change you've delayed for more than a year? What's the first step you could take this week to move toward it?

2. Who taught you how to shake hands, make eye contact, and carry yourself? What lessons did they instill that you still use today?

3. When in your life did someone claim you, choose you, when they didn't have to? How did that change you?

Me and Pops—love, laughter, and the first corner I ever knew.

Before I understood the fight, I was already built for it.

My mom, Pops, and me—the beginning of my story.

Pops, my mom, my sisters, and me—the early years.

THE MAKING OF A FIGHTER

"Discipline is what faith looks like when it's tired."

Every environment presents its own fights. The key is knowing when to avoid conflict, when to stand your ground, and when to detach. Chicago and Pleasant Grove in Dallas, the two places I bounced between growing up, weren't exactly safe or full of opportunities in those days, and not much has changed. What was meant to be a better place often felt like another battleground, where survival skills were as important as schoolwork.

Those years found me caught between two worlds: defending myself against kids in Dallas and resisting my family's expectations in Chicago. I didn't know who I was supposed to be in either place, so I just tried to blend in and hoped nobody noticed how unsure I felt.

By grade-school age, life with Pops had its own rhythm. He didn't punch a clock like other dads; he moved on his own terms. Money always showed up somehow, and I never went without. When he was out handling business or out living his own life, my aunts kept things steady. They made sure I was fed, dressed, and out of trouble. Between Pops' hustle and my aunts' care, I had structure, even when everything looked chaotic from the outside. Half the time I pretended I understood the routine, but really, I was just trying not to fall behind.

Pops expected me to handle mine. He never shook me awake for school or checked my homework, that was on me. He believed I was capable, even when my report cards said otherwise. But at night, he'd talk to me, dropping lessons that stuck longer than anything a teacher said. He wanted me to aim higher than the life he knew, to build something solid, to do right by my own family one day. I wanted to live up to that, even when I wasn't sure I had what it took.

School was where things started to crumble. No matter how hard Pops tried, sometimes pulling in whoever he was dating at the time to help me study, I just couldn't keep up. Watching my friends move on while I stayed behind was rough. Every time someone else advanced, it felt like proof that something was wrong with me.

Eventually, Pops figured a change might help, and he pulled me out of Nathaniel Hawthorne and put me in a private Christian school, hoping the new environment would do what he couldn't teach at home. That's where I met Mrs. Ruby, one of my favorite teachers ever. She tried everything to help me, but nothing clicked. Before they could hold me back again, the school shut down.

Before I learned how to fight, I had to learn how to take a hit.

Pops moved me to another private school, Temple Christian, and if I thought the first place was tough, this one was brutal. They dropped me straight into second grade even though I'd never officially passed first. Teachers told Pops they couldn't figure out what was wrong with me. Before long, they kicked me out, and I was back at square one.

I remember pretending it didn't bother me, but inside I felt like I kept failing tests I didn't know how to study for. I didn't want to return to Nathaniel Hawthorne, so Pops sent me up to Chicago to live with my Aunt Jackie and Uncle Curt along with my cousins Lil Curt, Twaan, and Marc. That school year turned into another disaster. I still hadn't officially passed first grade, yet somehow the school placed me in fifth based on my age, not my skills. Reading, writing, even following directions felt impossible. It was like being dropped into a race that had started years before I even showed up.

Living with my favorite cousin made it worse. He was sharp, so advanced that even though he was younger, he ran circles around me mentally. We'd do homework together, and every time I wrote something, he would ask his mom, "Why does Tony write like that? Why does he read like that? What's wrong with him?"

Aunt Jackie shut him down fast. I don't remember her exact words, but she made sure I didn't feel smaller than I already did. She stood up for me, made me feel seen. That was the first time I realized someone other than Pops and Aunt San believed in me. I didn't know how to say it, but that tiny bit of protection meant more than she probably realized.

I loved those summers running with my cousins at Aunt Jackie and Uncle Curt's. So even though school was tough, I was excited to be there. Still, I often felt overshadowed by how much further ahead they seemed. I looked up to my older cousin Twaan, the one everyone seemed to admire. He carried a confidence that made people pay attention. Being around him made me want to raise my own standard, even before I knew how to get there.

At the same time, I saw how heavy that spotlight could be. Marc carried a lot of expectations from the people around him, and sometimes you could see the weight of that. That's when I started to realize, you can't live your life trying to be somebody else. But that didn't stop me from wishing I had even a piece of what he had.

Marc was my favorite cousin. Even younger, he always looked out for me when I came to Chicago. When we were in elementary school together in Riverdale, he stepped in for me at a moment that really mattered. I was in fifth grade; the side you wore your hat on told people which gang you claimed to. Somebody stepped to me, and Marc jumped in, letting him know I was from Texas and didn't know any better.

Even back then, their whole family carried a kind of attention and respect I admired. I wanted a piece of that recognition, some proof that I mattered too. Everything felt like a competition, and while Marc usually won, I'm thankful now because it pushed me. Back then it just felt like I was always coming in last, even in rooms full of people who loved me.

All that time in Chicago made me hungry for my own lane. I didn't want to be "the cousin from Dallas." I wanted my own respect. But it wasn't easy. In Chicago, I was goofy Tony, older, chubby, shy, awkward, while Marc was cool, calm, and mature. My cousins called me lame for years, and it messed with my confidence. But that pressure lit something inside me. It's one of the biggest reasons I got so serious about boxing later. I needed something that was mine, something nobody could tease or take away.

When I got back to Dallas, nothing about Pleasant Grove had gotten easier. I was back in sixth grade, still struggling, still trying to find my footing. One of my teachers once told my Aunt San that I'd probably end up a dropout because of my grades and the trouble I was getting into. That stung, but even then, I tried to see the good. I'd made real friends, and that counted for something. Even when school made me feel behind, friendship made me feel like I belonged somewhere.

One of those friends was my boy Mickey. In Pleasant Grove, it was mostly Blacks and Mexicans, and there was always tension between the two. But for some reason, I always had a connection with the Mexican kids at school. Mickey was one of them. We met in sixth grade and were inseparable from day one. Mickey was an artist, he'd tag any wall he could find, and he was fearless when it came to fighting. He'd swing first, ask questions later. We got into everything together: sneaking around, cracking jokes, testing limits. When the neighborhood kids went looking for trouble, Mickey was already in the middle of it. He was the kind of friend who made you feel brave just standing next to him.

Truth is, I followed more than I led in those days. Mickey and the others started stealing cars and breaking into houses. I wanted to be part of the crew, but I was too scared of jail, so I'd play lookout. It wasn't smart, but it felt like belonging until the night Mickey got himself killed at a house party in ninth grade. That loss hit hard. The whole neighborhood felt it. It made me realize how thin the line really was between a dare and a death sentence. Part of me knew it could've just as easily been me, and that thought stayed with me for years.

Another close friend was a kid we called Pooh, straight from the hood, loyal to the bone. I wasn't the fighting type, but Pooh always had my back. If someone talked trash or tried to start something, he'd shut it down before it reached me. He was a protector and babysitter rolled into one. While Pops worked, guys like Pooh kept me company. Later, when we were older, Pops would toss us pizza money, throw on a movie, and head out to handle business.

With all that unsupervised time, we got into plenty, fighting, smoking weed, watching things kids shouldn't watch. But even then, I could separate what I did from who I was. I knew deep down the stupid stuff didn't define me, it was just the world we were living in. Not everyone saw it that way, though. Pooh and a lot of the others never made that separation, and some of them are still stuck where we started. I didn't know it then, but that ability to separate myself from the chaos is what saved me later.

By some miracle, they moved me up to seventh grade, even though I didn't have a clue how I'd passed sixth. If school had been hard before, John B. Hood Middle School in Pleasant Grove was another level. It was one of the roughest junior highs around, and I had to fight almost every day just to get through it. For someone like me, already behind in reading and writing, trying to study while watching your back was a losing game. I hated that place. School wasn't just hard, it felt like another place where I couldn't win.

I was twelve when everything shifted. I'll never forget the day my Aunt San picked me up from school. She didn't have to say anything, her face told me something was wrong. Then she said it: Big Kev, the big-brother figure Pops had been mentoring, had been murdered by a kid only two years older than me. Nobody knew why. Maybe it was a beef over a girl, maybe an attempted robbery. All I knew was that he was gone.

The pain hit deep. The only time I'd seen Pops that broken was when his youngest brother, my Uncle Rodney, was killed the day before his twenty-first birthday. Losing people started to feel normal, and that scared me more than anything.

But life keeps moving, whether you're ready or not. Somehow, even in the middle of all that loss, I felt like God was trying to tell me something. Not long after Kevin's death, my Aunt San took me to a small church in Pleasant Grove. The pastor was up front, calling people forward for prayer. I didn't want to go, but she made me. The pastor started blessing people one by one, but when he reached me, he stopped.

"There's an anointing over you," he said. "An energy, a presence. Whatever you're doing, keep doing it, and God's going to bless you."

I was twelve years old, standing there thinking, Who, me?, the kid who could barely read or write? For the first time, I wondered if maybe God saw something in me that I couldn't yet see in myself.

Not long after that, I messed up bad. Pooh, his sister, and I were hanging out at the rec center when she got into it with another girl. They fought, the other girl ran home, and we chased her all the way there. Trying to look cool, I kicked the door open, saw an apple on the counter, and threw it at her brother. It didn't register until later that the moment I kicked that door open, I'd crossed a line that could've caught me a breaking-and-entering charge.

We laughed the whole way back, right up until we saw three or four police cars waiting. The cops were checking the bottoms of everyone's shoes. When I kicked that door, I'd left a perfect print from my brand-new Dennis Rodman sneakers, the only pair like them in the neighborhood. I might as well have signed my name on that door.

By the time they got to me, I was a nervous wreck. They looked down, saw the pattern, and that was it. Next thing I knew, I was cuffed in the back of a patrol car, staring out the window at my friends, wondering how my life had flipped that fast. I remember thinking, This is it. This is where everything ends for me.

At the station, they sat me on a bench, still cuffed, head down, crying. Then Pops walked in. He went off, on me, on them, on the whole situation.

"This isn't who my son is," he said. "He's not one of these kids. I raised him by myself to be a man, and you'll never see him in here again, because he'll have to deal with me first."

They were supposed to put me on probation, maybe even send me to a reformatory school, but Pops wasn't having it. He tore up the paperwork right there. He fought so hard the officers actually stood up and clapped. We walked out together, no charges, no probation, but believe me, I never forgot that look in his eyes. I'd never felt more ashamed, or more protected, in my life.

Every punch I took in life taught me how to stand taller.

I knew better after that. I still failed seventh grade, and Pops decided to send me back to Chicago. For a stretch, I stayed with my aunt and uncle in the suburbs. The condo was nice, and it was exactly the fresh start I needed. It wasn't fancy, but it was stable—and at that time, stability mattered more than space. For the first time in a long time, I could focus on school without feeling like I had to watch my back every second. My aunt was a teacher, and she took my education personally. From the minute I arrived, she made it her mission to prove I didn't have a learning disability. She told me straight up, "You're not slow. You just haven't been taught right."

And she backed those words with action. When I needed to pass the Constitution test to graduate, she made it non-negotiable. Every day after school she'd drill me, locking me in the bathroom with the Constitution until I could recite sections from memory. Hours at a time, day after day, until I knew it inside out. To outsiders it might've looked harsh, maybe even abusive, but I knew her heart. She wasn't trying to punish me; she was trying to save me. And it worked. Whether her methods were right or wrong, they built something in me no textbook ever could, discipline and belief. When I finally passed that test, I felt proud for the first time in a long while. Aunt Shay is the reason I graduated, the reason I stopped believing I was broken. To this day, I thank God she cared enough to push me that hard. For once, I got to feel what winning something actually felt like.

For a while, I felt like I was finally getting somewhere, until I found out I couldn't stay. I had to go back to Pleasant Grove for high school. It hurt to leave, but I carried what she taught me back with me.

The irony is, plenty of people doubted Pops could raise me alone, a kid with learning issues and social awkwardness. They thought I'd be the one to end up behind bars. What they didn't see was the hunger underneath all that chaos. No matter where I lived or who was around me, I knew there was more out there waiting. And I was determined to reach it. Even when I didn't know the path, I knew I couldn't afford to stop moving.

What I didn't know yet was that the next lesson wouldn't come from the streets, it would come from a teacher who saw more in me than I saw in myself.

REFLECTIONS

YOUR START ISN'T YOUR FINISH

> *Where you start doesn't decide where you finish.*
> *Love, structure, and purpose can rewrite any origin story.*

Your environment shapes you, but it doesn't have to determine your outcome. I didn't grow up with the perfect home setup. Being raised by a single father came with its share of challenges, but I was surrounded by love and support from my Pops' sisters, who helped raise me and made sure my education stayed on track.

My mom's absence could have been the reason I failed, but it became part of why I succeeded. Pops was grounded in his purpose, and even though he wasn't perfect, he made sure I had the structure I needed. My mother, on the other hand, was young and still trying to figure life out. I didn't understand it as a kid, but now I can see she was doing the best she could with what she knew.

Those different environments, some steady, some shaky, taught me not to let where I come from limit where I can go.

THE STRUGGLE WAS REAL

> *Hard beginnings build discipline.*
> *Every setback is practice for getting back up stronger.*

I never wanted to be "that kid", the one teachers whispered about, the one who had to start over while everybody else moved on. Every time I thought I was catching up, life threw another curve, a school closed, a teacher gave up, or I just couldn't keep up no matter how hard I tried.

I didn't understand why learning felt like a fight. I thought maybe something was wrong with me. But all those setbacks became my training ground. Getting held back, switching schools, watching friends pass me by, it all taught me how to keep showing up when it would've been easier to quit.

Looking back, I realize that was the start of the fighter in me. I was learning discipline before I ever put on gloves. The lessons didn't come from books; they came from getting knocked down, standing back up, and doing it again until something finally stuck.

BE CAREFUL WHO YOU FOLLOW

> *Not every light leads forward.*
> *Choose purpose over popularity and let faith be your guide.*

When you grow up around people with big personalities, big dreams, and even bigger reputations, it's easy to start chasing what looks like success instead of what is success. I've seen how quick it can all flip, one decision, one bad influence, one moment where you follow the wrong voice instead of God's.

These days, I keep my eyes on what's eternal, not what's popular. The fame, the fortune, the street respect, none of it means anything if you lose yourself chasing it. Every day, I remind myself to follow the One who led me out when others didn't make it.

LUCKY TO BE ALIVE

> *Loss reminds us to live fully.*
> *Surviving means carrying forward the best of those who didn't.*

I've lost more friends than some people have ever been fortunate enough to have. Big Kev. Mickey. Others whose names I still carry with me. No matter the reason or when it happened, each loss leaves a mark on you, especially when you start to realize it could have been you on any one of those occasions. Growing up with so much loss has given me more perspective on just how fortunate I am to be alive and makes me want to live life to the fullest. I could have held a grudge or felt the need to avenge their murders and landed myself in jail or dead, but I've always tried to carry forward the good memories. That perspective keeps me grounded and grateful, which is exactly why I'm including this section.

TEACHER AND STUDENT

> *Learning works both ways.*
> *Stay humble enough to learn and wise enough to teach.*

There are very few things we learn completely on our own. Even as babies, despite having the natural urge to walk, we always have someone nearby to help, someone to catch us, cushion the fall, or cheer when we finally stand. Learning from someone who's mastered a craft should make things easier, but it can be just as hard when teacher and student don't connect.

I wasn't a great student in school, and now I see those struggles as preparation. Growth takes humility, from both sides. The best teachers adjust; the best students stay open. Sometimes you need more than one teacher, and that's okay. Later in boxing, I'd go to my mentor when I was struggling with something my coach was showing me, and he'd break it down simply. Once I got it, I could go back and master it. No one took offense. We all became better teachers and students because of it.

NOTHING IS BENEATH A WINNER

> *Greatness starts in the grind.*
> *No task is too small when it builds the foundation for a dream.*

I started taking school seriously once I realized how much it mattered to my boxing career. I earned my two-year degree in just under four years while still working at the apartments that provided my housing. The administration helped me take just enough classes to stay eligible so I could keep training and living rent-free.

No one forced me to do that. I could've quit, like a lot of people did when things got hard. But the grind taught me something important: winners don't wait for easy conditions, they create opportunity out of what's in front of them. Every mop I pushed, every late night studying, built the foundation for everything I've done since.

CORNER QUESTIONS

1. When did you first realize your environment was trying to define you?

2. What's one fight you're choosing that God's already told you to walk away from?

3. Who in your circle pushes you to grow, and who just pulls you back to old habits?

My Chicago cousins—love, pressure, and the fight to earn respect.

Back home in Pleasant Grove—family, roots, and a different kind of fight.

Graduation day—proof I could finish what I started.

Pleasant Grove—sixth grade, trying to fit in before I knew who I was.

BETWEEN TROUBLE AND A TEACHER

"Sometimes God sends correction disguised as consequence."

The struggle isn't with other people, it's with pain itself. Forgiving my past didn't make me weak, it made me stronger.

When I moved back to Pleasant Grove, I had just spent time watching my cousin Twaan do everything right. He was disciplined, focused, and the kind of athlete people admired, earning opportunities most kids only dream about. Being around him made me see every place I still felt behind, even when I tried to laugh it off.

One night, after we watched the movie *Life*, he looked over at me and joked, "Man, you Tony 'Can't Get Right' Mack." In *Life*, "Can't Get Right" is the guy who can't do anything right, so when my cousin said it, it hit like a real label, not just a joke. I laughed with him, but inside, it stung. A part of me believed it, especially during a time when everything felt like it was falling apart and I couldn't seem to get anything right. I didn't say it out loud, but hearing that nickname made something settle heavy in my chest, like maybe he was just saying what I already feared.

I've said before that some of the schools I went to were rough and that I hung around guys who lived the thug life, but I need to be clear about how much worse things had gotten by the time I went back to attend Samuell High School in Pleasant Grove at fifteen. It wasn't just tough; it was chaos on repeat. I'd been away for about a year, and coming back felt like walking straight into a fight that never stopped. Part of me wondered if maybe I had changed, or if I was just finally seeing the place for what it really was.

That's when everything hit the fan. I joined a gang, UPT, which stood for Umphress Park Texas, with Pooh and his big brother. We didn't do it because it sounded cool; we did it because we were tired of being targets. Big Kev had started the gang years before he was killed, and the older guys kept it going after he was gone. We followed suit for protection.

Funny thing was, it never felt safe. We were constantly fighting rival gangs, getting shot at, jumped, and watching friends die. My boys were stealing everything from school projectors to Hyundais. I was always there when it went down, but I never joined in, not because I thought I was better, but because I was terrified of what Pops would do if I ever got caught. Fear of disappointing him was the only thing that kept me from crossing a line I knew I couldn't come back from.

I wasn't built for the streets; I was built to outgrow them

Even though I stayed out of trouble with the law, life on the streets didn't feel much better. Every day was survival. If Pooh was around, I felt protected; when he wasn't, I had to watch my back. It didn't matter whether I was walking the halls at school or just heading to the corner store, somebody was always ready to test you. I started skipping school more than I showed up. Pops thought I was there every day, and technically I was, at least for roll call. I'd walk into class, sit for a few minutes, then head back out to the streets to meet up with my friends. I knew I was drifting, but I didn't know how to pull myself back yet.

The summer after I failed ninth grade, I stayed with my cousin Big Reese, his girlfriend at the time, and her son. Out of all my cousins, Big Reese was one of my favorites, so when they offered to let me live with them and switch to North Dallas schools, I jumped at it. For a minute, it felt like a new beginning, new neighborhood, new rhythm, maybe even a chance to finally get right. But it didn't last. Pops didn't like the idea of me living under another man's roof, especially one with a girlfriend and kid. And not long after, Big Reese moved out, which meant I'd have to go back to Pleasant Grove, exactly what I didn't want. Every time I thought I'd found a way out, something dragged me right back to where I'd started.

Things shifted when Big Reese was no longer living there. After that, his mom, my Aunt San, moved into his condo. She had just come back from Chicago, and having a stable place gave her a fresh start. Once she was settled, I asked if I could stay with her too, and thankfully she said yes.

That condo changed everything for me. It sat just one block inside the Plano school-district line. Literally one block. If it had been on the Dallas side, I would've gone right back into the same environment I'd been struggling in. But because Aunt San was living in Big Reese's old place, I suddenly had access to schools in Plano, a completely different world from what I was used to. For the first time, it felt like maybe life wasn't just happening to me, maybe something was shifting in my favor.

That's how I ended up in the Plano school system. Not because of a plan, not because someone mapped out my future, but because my aunt moved into her son's condo when he wasn't home anymore, and the address landed on the "right" side of the line. One change in my family opened a door I never would have walked through otherwise. It wasn't some dramatic turning point—just a lucky break that gave me room to breathe. And at that age, that was enough to feel like hope.

That summer could've gone a whole different way. The streets were getting darker every day, and so were some of my friends.

One of my friends, Ben, and another friend we all hung with stole a pit bull and traded it for a sawed-off shotgun. Ben was a few years older, and that friend, well, he was more about the thug lifestyle than any of us. I remember one day when we were riding bikes together, that same friend told me straight up that he was going to kill somebody before he made it to high school. I brushed it off because I'd known him since first grade. He was one of my good friends, and I didn't see that side of him the way others did. Looking back, I realize how blinded I was by loyalty, by history, by wanting to believe my friends were better than the choices they were making.

That summer, when my Pops, Ben, Pooh, and another friend from the Grove helped move my stuff into my Aunt San's house, I didn't know it would be the last time I'd ever see Ben or that friend together. Just a week later, everything changed.

I was with Ben the week before the shooting, and for once, we weren't joking around or clowning each other. He was actually complimenting me, telling me how grown up I was getting. He'd noticed I'd been in the weight room, putting in work for football season, and he told me he was proud of me. Ben, the same dude who used to bully all of us, was giving me props. It felt good, like maybe I was finally earning his respect. And then, just like that, he was gone forever. I kept replaying that conversation in my head, wondering how a week could hold both the best and worst version of someone you love.

That same friend who had helped steal the pit bull was still around, but not for long. He was about to be taken out of my life too, facing a murder conviction that would have him locked up until he was twenty-one. In the span of a day, I lost two of my best friends, one to the grave, one to the system. It was the first time I really understood that "forever" could end in a single moment.

Here's what happened. Ben was older and stronger than most of us, and he had this way of pushing us around. Most of the time, we didn't take it personally. That was just Ben. But for whatever reason, that day, he pushed too far. The friend had been holding onto the shotgun they traded for the pit bull, and Ben decided he wanted it for himself. He went over to that friend's house, where the friend's mom and a few of our other boys were hanging out. He started bullying him, trying to take the gun, and from what everyone said later, you could see the fear in that kid's face.

Then it happened. One second, they were yelling. The next, a shot rang out. Ben was hit in the neck and dropped right there in front of everyone. Dead before he hit the ground.

When I got the call, I couldn't believe it. I thank God I wasn't there to see it. If I'd been standing in that room, I don't know how much worse it would've messed me up. It already changed me enough as it was. That day showed me how fast life can turn. One bad decision, one heated moment, and it's over. It was the first time I understood that survival wasn't guaranteed, not even for the strongest among us.

Of all the things I'd seen up to that point, the fights, the fear, the funerals, that one broke something in me. It was the first time I really understood what it meant to lose somebody before they ever had a chance to grow.

Aunt Shay didn't just teach me, she saved me. Her lessons hurt sometimes, but so does growth.

When I was in my second year of ninth grade, yeah, another repeat year, at Pleasant Grove, the school rolled out this new thing called the Bellwether program. I didn't understand what it was at the time, but looking back, I think they meant well. From what I've learned since, Bellwether was a national nonprofit focused on transforming education for kids like me, students from rough backgrounds or with learning challenges.

On paper, it sounded good. In reality, it was something else entirely. The school put us in portable classrooms behind the main building, partly because the school was overcrowded, partly because they wanted to keep "our kind" grouped together. It was supposed to help us catch up. Instead, it felt like they'd just given up on us. Even then, I could feel the difference between being helped and being hidden.

If you've ever seen *Dangerous Minds* with Michelle Pfeiffer, that's about as close as you can get to what those days looked like. The fighting never stopped. The teachers had no control, and most didn't even try after a while. When they were in the room, they'd get so frustrated they'd start yelling at the kids. And when they stepped out, to grab a folder, go to the office, or use the bathroom, it turned into a full-blown circus.

I remember one day a friend brought in a VHS tape and hijacked the class VCR so we could all watch *Baller Blockin'*, a hood movie starring a young Lil Wayne and the Hot Boys. It had no business being shown in a school, but that was the Bellwether life: no rules, no order, no direction.

Then there were the fights. Every day you had a chance of getting jumped, and the portables didn't make things any safer. If someone wanted to fight, they did, and you had no choice but to swing back. That's how I got my first black eye. I don't even remember what started it, but one of the kids was whooping me pretty good. His knee was about to crash down on my head when Pooh came flying out of nowhere and tackled him off me. I didn't even know Pooh was on campus that day, but thank God he was, because no one else was jumping in. Moments like that made me realize how close I always was to losing, not just fights, but myself.

That was the kind of environment we were living in, constant pressure, constant noise. You couldn't learn even if you wanted to. But underneath all that chaos, something was changing in me. I started realizing that if I was going to make it out, it had to come from me. Nobody was coming to save me, not the school, not the system, not the streets. It was the first time I heard that quiet voice inside saying, "You have to want more than this."

During that same time, I ended up beefing with a rival gang called N.A.B. To this day, I don't even remember what started it. Maybe something I said, maybe a look, maybe nothing at all. But before I knew it, word got around that their leader, one of the toughest dudes in school, was looking for me. He wanted to fight, and everyone was talking about it.

I was terrified. I'd been in plenty of fights before, but this was different. He was built, and I was worn out, physically, mentally, emotionally. The last thing I wanted was another fight, but that's what life in Pleasant Grove was: nonstop survival mode. You didn't have to look for a fight; it always found you. I remember thinking, "I don't know how much more of this I can take."

Then, almost like divine timing, I found out I was moving to Plano. It wasn't planned to escape Pleasant Grove or N.A.B., but it sure felt like God was stepping in right when I needed a break. I'm not saying he ran me out of town, it was just one of those twists of fate that probably saved me from something worse. For the first time in a long time, I felt relief, like maybe I'd finally been given a chance to breathe.

When my cousin gave me that nickname, Tony "Can't Get Right" Mack, I believed it for a long time. I really thought that was who I was: the kid who couldn't get school right, couldn't stay out of trouble, couldn't figure life out. But standing here now, looking back on everything that came after, the fights, the failures, the funerals, I can finally see it for what it was. It wasn't about getting it right. It was about getting through. I survived things that should've taken me out, I just didn't know yet that surviving was also a kind of winning.

The blessing that the pastor spoke over me years earlier wasn't some miracle waiting to fall out of the sky. It was already inside me, showing up in those moments I somehow survived when I shouldn't have. I didn't see it then, but every round I made it through in Pleasant Grove was proof that God was still in my corner.

Everything Aunt Shay planted was starting to grow, even if I didn't see it yet. I wasn't "Can't Get Right." I was becoming someone who refused to stay down.

I was just getting ready.

REFLECTIONS

LOOK TO THE FUTURE, NOT THE PAST

> *Forgiveness frees you.*
> *Let go of what hurt you so you can grow into who you're meant to be.*

One of the hardest things I've had to do is look at my relationship with my mother through a different lens. By the time I was in Plano, I'd stopped blaming my mom. I realized she was surviving just like I was. As a kid, I couldn't understand how a mother could walk away, and sometimes I wondered if it was my fault. Maybe that's why I got so over-the-top excited whenever she showed up, even for something small. It used to bother my Pops. He did everything for me day in and day out, and I didn't show the same excitement for him. But that's just how kids are, we crave what we feel we're missing.

As I've grown, I've come to realize my mom didn't leave out of malice or neglect; she was doing the best she could to play the hand she was dealt. Understanding that has given me peace and allowed me to forgive.

OUTGROWING YOUR ROOTS

> *You can love where you came from and still outgrow it.*
> *Protect your peace as you rise.*

I'm not sure what it is, but I've definitely thought about going back to the old hood and seeing how some of my friends are doing. I never make it there, though, because, honestly, I'm a little uncomfortable about reconnecting with the guys back in Pleasant Grove. They're struggling and hurting, and they all know I'm doing well. I don't like to think they'd ever do anything to me, but when someone's at their lowest point, you can never be too careful.

Back then I had nothing to lose; now I have a house, a wife, and a thriving business built on the brand I fought to create. I'll always love where I came from, it made me who I am, but sometimes growth means loving people from a distance.

ASSUME YOU BELONG

> *Confidence isn't given, it's claimed.*
> *Step into every room like you earned your spot.*

My cousin called me "Can't Get Right," and for years, I let that define me. I assumed I didn't belong in rooms where everyone else seemed to have it together. But belonging isn't about being perfect, it's about showing up even when you feel behind. The moment I stopped apologizing for where I'd been and started owning where I was going, everything changed.

It's hard to believe you belong when the people closest to you are already stars. One of my cousins was the kind of athlete everyone talked about, dominant, disciplined, and destined for big things. In our family, that level of success made you a legend. When you grow up around people like that, it's easy to feel like you're standing in their shadow.

For a long time, I didn't think I measured up. I was the goofy one, the slow learner, the kid always trying to catch up. What I didn't understand back then was that their shine didn't take anything away from mine. I just had to show up, put in the work, and earn my own light. Once I stopped comparing myself to everyone else and started moving with confidence, I finally felt like I belonged, not because of what they achieved, but because of who I was becoming.

THE ROAD TO HELL IS PAVED WITH GOOD INTENTIONS

> *Even "helpful" systems can trap people.*
> *True change starts when you question the setup, not just the student.*

The Bellwether program started by building all-new "classrooms" outside the main school building in portable containers. They broke us up by age and learning level and assigned us to those rooms. We had a group of kids who were already struggling, cutting class, barely attending, and now we were isolated from everyone else.

Most of the students selected for Bellwether were considered impossible to teach or control within the confines of the main building, which was already like a prison. What could possibly go wrong by moving them outside with less supervision, right? It was meant to help, but it only made things worse. Good intentions don't mean good results.

LIFE IS A MARATHON, NOT A SPRINT

> *Progress takes patience. The slow climb builds endurance*
> *and gratitude that shortcuts never will.*

It's not where you start that defines you, but where you finish. To reach your destination, discipline and belief are essential. Starting from the bottom gave me a clear view of the top. I learned to tune out the noise of those who quit early and keep climbing. I used to hate school, but I discovered a love for learning once I focused on it. Reading felt like punishment because I wasn't good at it, but now it feels like power. I often heard, "If you want to hide something from a Black man, put it in a book." Today, books are my source of truth. Ironically, I'm more successful than those who once seemed ahead. Professors and business owners seek my advice. The kid who struggled with reading and math now owns a world-class boxing gym and leads others. Patience, faith, and endurance built this. Life really is a marathon.

CORNER QUESTIONS

1. What would forgiving someone really change for you, not them?

2. What part of your past are you still fighting even though the real opponent is long gone?

3. What lesson did struggle teach you that comfort never could?

W.W. Samuell High School football squad, Pleasant Grove—I'm number 62, still trying to find my place before life ever put gloves on me.

Where school felt temporary—and trouble didn't.

The park where survival was normal—and discipline had to be chosen.

With my cousins—learning where I fit, and where I didn't.

FINDING MY CORNER

"Trust is earned one round at a time."

Before I learned how to throw a punch, I learned to trust the process. Faith wasn't just about belief, it was about moving forward in the dark. Plano didn't magically fix me; it just gave me room to breathe. No metal detectors, no constant ambushes, just halls that didn't suffocate me, a seat in a resource class I finally stopped sneaking into, and the difficult decision to repeat instead of pretending. I worked like a starter who never actually played, letting the effort be my proof. For the first time, the world got quiet enough for me to hear what I really wanted.

My Aunt San's condo happened to sit one block on the right side of the school-district line, which let me attend Shepton High School in Plano instead of North Dallas, thank God, because that place wasn't much better than Pleasant Grove. Shepton was almost entirely White, and there I was: a Black kid who had been left back so many times he barely knew what was going on. They placed me in special-needs classes, hoping it would help me learn. It was embarrassing, but as I'd later realize, it turned out to be one of the best things that ever happened to me. I hated feeling behind, but I knew I couldn't fake my way through another year.

When I got to high school in Plano, talk about me joining the football team started up naturally, even though nobody had ever seen me play. A few things worked in my favor, including having family members who already had a solid reputation. First, I had a positive attitude, which made it easy to fit in with different crowds. Second, I was still big for my age and one of the only Black kids in the school, so people assumed I had some kind of football talent. Third, I'd built a close bond with the only Black coach on staff, and he wanted me out there. And last, but probably most important, was my belief that if I wanted to be on that team, not making the cut wasn't even an option. I couldn't imagine a world where I tried out and didn't get picked. I needed something to belong to, even if I didn't know where I fit yet.

Notice I said "picked," not "played." That's because this was one of those times when assumptions, both theirs and mine, couldn't have been further from the truth. I was too small for defense and didn't have the skill for offense. On junior varsity, I got a few snaps here and there, but no matter how much or little I played, I built a reputation as one of the hardest workers on the team. I showed up on time to every practice, never missed a day, and left my heart on the field because I knew it helped my teammates get better.

Belonging doesn't have to come from being the best. Sometimes your role is to show up, work hard, and cheer for the people who do get on the field.

On paper, I never should've made varsity, but I did.

If I thought JV meant little playing time, varsity was worse. Practice was the only time I touched the field. We had a running joke whenever someone asked what position I played: "ass back." You might think I meant "halfback," but no, whenever I asked the coach if I could go in, he'd say, "Boy, get your ass back on the bench!"

It never bothered me. Against all odds, I still felt part of the team and made a lot of great friends in the process. Just being included felt new to me, and I didn't want to lose it.

On the outside, I looked like a regular student who played football to earn respect. Inside, I was learning something bigger: belonging doesn't have to come from being the best. Sometimes your role is to show up, work hard, and cheer for the people who do get on the field. That still counts.

At the same time, being in special education classes was tough to swallow. After everything I'd already been through, it felt like one more reminder that I was behind. But that room in the back of the school forced me to slow down long enough to actually learn instead of just survive.

I remember one of the biggest and most embarrassing moments of my life happening in tenth grade at Shepton. Everybody knew who the special education students were. Even as the new kid, I knew it wouldn't take long for people to figure it out about me. To hide it, I started going to class fifteen or twenty minutes late so my friends wouldn't see me walking into the special ed room. Most of them thought I was smarter than I really was, probably because I had a high social IQ and could talk my way through anything.

But one day my friend Darius saw me sitting in class with two of the well-known special ed kids, and he made sure everyone knew. I don't think he meant it to be mean; he was more surprised than anything, but that didn't matter. I was mortified. I thought everyone's perception of me would change overnight. But it didn't. I waited for people to clown me, but nobody did, and that threw me off.

The friendships I made in Plano taught me something I didn't expect. The guys in my circle didn't care about the label or the class I was in. They supported me, helped me figure out what courses to take, how to make up credits, and what it would take to get back on track to graduate on time in 2003 and move up to Plano West, where I belonged. If it weren't for those friends, I don't know that I would've worked as hard as I did to catch up.

But none of that would have happened if I hadn't made one of the hardest choices of my life: I chose to repeat tenth grade on purpose.

Saying no to advancing with my friends was brutal, especially after all those years of trying to fit in and prove I wasn't slow. But deep down, I knew I wasn't ready. For the first time, I stopped pretending. I decided to stay behind, get it right, and actually learn. It felt like admitting I'd failed, but it was really the first time I told the truth about where I was.

That choice changed everything.

I couldn't imagine leaving an environment where everyone around me was so kind, patient, and genuinely wanted to see me win. They didn't want anything from me in return; they just wanted me to grow. Being around those people and making that decision shifted something in me. If I'd moved forward before I was ready, I might never have graduated at all.

Life at Plano West was the total opposite of Pleasant Grove, like night and day. Going from metal detectors and daily police patrols to total freedom felt unreal. At Samuell, once you were inside, you stayed locked in until the bell rang. At Plano West, you could leave campus for lunch every day. Instead of friends riding the bus and robbing people on weekends, I was surrounded by kids driving BMWs and hanging out at house parties that looked straight out of a movie. It felt like stepping into a world I'd only seen on TV and never imagined I'd be part of.

Before I got there, I thought *American Pie* and *Clueless* were Hollywood exaggerations, but suddenly I was living them. Somehow, I'd manifested that world, and before long, I was hanging with those same kinds of kids. No one at Plano West saw me as the "slow" kid or the "outsider." I was respected, and for the first time in my life, that came without me having to fight for it. I could just be myself, no mask, no act. That new environment did more for my confidence than any classroom ever could. It felt good to breathe without looking over my shoulder.

One of the first things I noticed about the theater crowd was how comfortable they were being themselves. Everybody was relaxed, funny, and real. We were all like family. I'll never forget the first time we were backstage getting into costume and the girls started changing right in front of us. My jaw probably hit the floor. That would've never happened back in my old world, but here, it was normal. Around the theater kids, I felt like I could finally breathe. I didn't have to act like someone else to fit in, even though we were literally acting every day.

The drama community was so diverse and full of energy that I couldn't help being drawn in. My first show was *Guys and Dolls* in tenth grade, where I didn't even have lines. But by junior year, I auditioned for *Grease* and landed the role of Johnny Casino, a solo singing part complete with the "hand jive" dance. Only, I kept calling it the "hand job" by mistake. You can imagine how that went over. Everybody laughed, but I rolled with it, and when the curtain went up, I crushed that performance. For once, the spotlight didn't scare me; it felt like home.

Then came the Class President announcement in eleventh grade. I was sitting in class when they said anyone interested should report to the auditorium. Nothing like that had ever crossed my mind before, but something told me to go. I turned to my friend and said, "I think I'm gonna run." He looked at me like I'd lost it. "Man, Tony," he said, "ain't none of these White people gonna vote for your Black, broke, ugly ass." Hearing that should've shut me down, but something in me wouldn't let it.

He meant it as a joke, but it lit a fire in me. I went home and told my Aunt San I wanted to run, and she didn't hesitate to believe in me. She helped me build my campaign from scratch, kept me on top of my grades, helped me craft my speech, and made sure I had something real to say.

We filled the halls with posters listing my reasons for running. I was up against the school's valedictorian and a few of the "who's who" of Plano West, but I never let that shake me. Deep down, I wanted to prove I belonged in rooms I used to be scared to walk into.

Then, on election day, one of my friends pointed out that every poster we'd hung, hundreds of them, had a word misspelled. I thought it was over right there. But either nobody noticed or they didn't care. When they announced the winner, it wasn't even close. I won by a landslide. Hearing my name called felt unreal, like my whole story flipped in one second. For a second, I thought maybe my football buddies scared people into voting for me, but I realized it was bigger than that. People saw my heart.

After I won Class President, the panic set in. I was proud, but terrified. I didn't even know what the job was supposed to be. Part of me never believed I'd actually win, but there I was, with everyone watching. My family was so proud. My folks in Chicago couldn't believe it: the same kid who'd once struggled to spell now winning elections in an all-White school. And that spelling mistake? It became part of the legend. I kept wondering if they'd eventually figure out I was still catching up.

Being Class President came with perks I never saw coming. They moved me from special education into mostly regular classes, and even some advanced classes. When it came time for tests, I still took them in a separate room with extra help, but that shift mattered. It meant people believed I could hang.

Then came Homecoming. I hadn't planned to run for King, but someone must've written my name down, and next thing I knew, I was standing there with a crown next to the captain of the cheerleading squad, and one of the most popular girls in school. The crazy part? We were both Black. In a school where less than ten percent of students looked like us, that win meant something bigger than either of us realized. We even ended up featured in The Dallas Morning News. Seeing that picture made me feel like I'd stepped into a life I never knew was possible for me.

Funny enough, when Prom rolled around, I wasn't even allowed to run for King. The school said it wouldn't be fair because I'd already "won enough." I laughed it off, but inside, I couldn't believe it. Me, the same kid who used to hide outside classrooms, was now the one they said couldn't lose.

Then came "Mr. West," the school's talent show where the winner got the crown. I didn't hesitate. Acting had already given me confidence I never knew I had, and I wanted to show out. I decided to perform Andre 3000's "Hey Ya!" and convinced my football buddies to play the rest of the band. We went all in, guitars, drums, everything, and I even borrowed my Aunt San's wig to pull off the look. By the end of the night, we had the whole place on its feet. For the first time, I felt like I could walk into a room and make it mine.

All of that led to graduation, my biggest stage yet. Out of thousands of students, I was chosen to be the master of ceremonies. The ceremony was held at the Dallas Convention Center, and as I stood there looking out over that sea of faces, it hit me: a kid who once struggled to read was now delivering the speech of his life. My Aunt San and my English teacher Mrs. Townsend worked with me for weeks to get every word perfect. To this day, people still tell me it was one of the best speeches they've ever heard. Standing at that podium felt like every setback had finally paid off.

That moment, and everything that came before it, changed me forever. Winning Class President, performing on stage, giving that speech, it all built the confidence that carried me into every fight, every risk, every chapter that came next.

It gave me the courage to start from scratch after graduation. To try boxing when I had no idea what I was doing. To believe that even if I started late, I could still win big. I finally believed I could build something from nothing.

Late blooming became my secret weapon. Watching from behind taught me patience. Struggling taught me humility. Failing taught me faith.

Late blooming became my secret weapon. Watching from behind taught me patience. Struggling taught me humility. Failing taught me faith. Most people rush to "get there." Me? I learned that life isn't about rushing, it's about rhythm. I'm not perfect. I don't always have it figured out. But when I'm alone, I'm my biggest competition. And I keep winning. God keeps putting the right people in my corner at the right time, guiding me through the next fight. As I step into my new roles, author, promoter, and teacher, I still feel like the outsider. But that's exactly why I know I'll succeed. Being the outsider has always pushed me to rise instead of fold. By the time I was wearing a crown, cracking jokes in Andre's wig, and speaking at graduation, I'd already learned how to win without stats. I wasn't the best athlete. I wasn't the smartest kid in the room. But I was learning how to belong without performing, and that changed everything. I finally had footing, even if I didn't know the path yet.

I'd climbed out of the corner, but life was about to ring the next bell. After the cap and gown, that's where the next fight began.

REFLECTIONS

ACTING FOR AUTHENTICITY

> *Sometimes the smallest role reveals your purpose.*
> *Faith uses unlikely scenes to set your stage.*

Throughout my life, God has given me numerous signs about what to do with my life, even when I didn't recognize them in the moment. One of those signs came in tenth grade at Shepton High School, when I auditioned for the play Guys and Dolls. I'd always wanted to perform, to be in front of people, so I took a leap of faith and landed the role, the nameless boxer.

Preparing for that opening scene, my only scene in the entire play, was the first time I ever laced up boxing gloves. I didn't have any lines, and outside of strutting across the stage in that gear, my part was small. But that moment sparked something in me. I fell in love with performing and realized later it was more than acting, it was foreshadowing. God was already showing me where I belonged.

WHO WOULD HAVE THOUGHT?

> *Never count yourself out.*
> *What once felt impossible becomes the story everyone remembers.*

When I ran for Class President, I had no idea the job came with organizing the ten-, twenty-, and thirty-year reunions. If I'd known, I might've backed out. I could barely read back then, how was I supposed to plan events? None of my classmates believed I could do it, and I spent years convinced I'd let everyone down.

But the fear was all in my head. I hosted both reunions at high-end venues, and the turnout and feedback were incredible. The twenty-year reunion even outshined the ten-year. People who once doubted me were shocked, and proud. Now I just have to top it for the thirty-year. The kid who once struggled to read now brings people together. Who would've thought?

BE THANKFUL

> *Gratitude resets your spirit.*
> *Even the hard days hold blessings when you look close enough.*

No matter what you expect, life will still hit you fast sometimes. When it does, you can't take yourself too seriously. You have to step back and stay grateful for what you do have. I've had plenty of bad things happen over the years, but every one of them could've been worse. It didn't feel like that at the time, and some people might think I'm saying this now only because I've had success. That couldn't be further from the truth.

Not a day goes by that I don't think about the reasons I'm where I am. It's easy to take things for granted when we see others still struggling, but that should make us even more grateful for our blessings. In hard seasons, a blessing can feel like a burden, but when you step back and imagine the alternative, gratitude shows up fast. It always has for me.

THRIVING AS AN OUTSIDER

> *Wanting to fit in is part of human nature.*
> *Feeling loved and accepted is a basic need.*

I wasn't alone growing up, I had friends, but I was still an outsider. I hung around guys who ran in packs but never really fit. Even at Plano West, I was still "the Black kid from Pleasant Grove" until I learned who I was. I was a late bloomer. My younger cousins were sharper and more mature, and I was often the oldest in class after being held back. Reading didn't click for me until almost thirty. That struggle taught me patience and made me realize my differences weren't weaknesses, they were part of my design.

I was late in a lot of areas in my life. Things other people seemed to figure out early took me longer, and for a long time I thought that meant something was wrong with me. Now I see it differently. Moving at my own pace kept me focused and protected me from crashing before I found discipline. What once made me feel "behind" became one of my biggest strengths.

STUDENT BECOMING THE TEACHER

> *Growth means shifting roles. When you've learned enough to guide others, even the ones who taught you, you honor them.*

When I think about everything I've accomplished, I sometimes feel guilty for how it's changed my relationship with my Pops. Growing up, he was my role model, the man who showed me how to hustle, take responsibility, and live life on my own terms.

But as I've grown, our roles have shifted. In some ways, I've become the teacher, the one showing him new perspectives. That's not easy for either of us, but it's part of growth. If I've learned anything from him, it's that real men never stop learning.

A HIGHER POWER

> *Faith keeps you steady through the tests of life. Trust the process, stay consistent, and keep working your corner.*

Growing up, I didn't think much about it, but now I see how faith shaped my outlook. Whether it's God, the universe, or energy, something bigger has always guided me. Those long church services, which I used to complain about, planted deep roots, teaching discipline, gratitude, and that even in unfair times, there's purpose.

I thank God when things go well, and when they don't, I keep faith. Life isn't meant to be easy; struggles prepare us for greater things. God doesn't want perfection, just readiness. Every challenge is training for something bigger. I believe the people who helped me along the way were there for a reason. My best advice: trust the process and God. There's a plan if you don't quit.

CORNER QUESTIONS

1. When was the last time you acted like you belonged before anyone said you did?

2. How often do you thank God for unanswered prayers that turned into blessings later?

3. What does "faith in motion" look like in your daily life?

Homecoming King in Plano—proof that a kid from Pleasant Grove could belong anywhere.

Juniors elect leader for next year

Preparing for Senior Class President 2004

"I just didn't want to be a regular senior," Mack said.

When my name hit print—and my confidence hit the next level.

Plano years—new circle, new standards, new expectations.

Homecoming night—confidence I didn't know I had became real.

PART II
FIGHT NIGHT

"You don't win under the lights,
you win in the dark, when no one's watching."

This is the part where the lights come on, and the noise gets loud. Every fighter learns fast that fight night only reveals what you practiced in silence. These rounds are about staying poised when adrenaline spikes, ego gets loud, and everything you've done in private gets tested in public.

Touching Olympic ground—a kid from Pleasant Grove standing under "USA," realizing the dream was real.

BLOOD, SWEAT AND SCORECARDS

"Effort is the only currency that always pays back."

Every fighter recalls the first true hit, the moment that reveals whether you love the fight itself or just the desire to win.

After Plano West and graduation, I felt completely lost, unsure of what path to follow. I knew I wasn't a top student, so pursuing academics seemed unlikely. As a nineteen-year-old, what I did know was that I didn't want to keep living with Aunt San, and I definitely wasn't going back to live with my Pops. I felt too old to still be stuck between other people's plans.

Community college seemed like the bridge between freedom and figuring it out. It gave me a place to live on my own and a reason to stay busy, even if school wasn't exactly what I was there for. I remembered how much I loved theater in high school, so I took a few liberal-arts courses just to stay eligible. I had to start at the bottom academically, but that didn't bother me. I just wanted to act again. So I enrolled in a few drama and acting classes at Collin County Community College. Deep down, I hoped something would finally stick.

Somehow, I landed a role in my first, and only, independent movie, *Vampire X*. I played the headmistress's vampire bodyguard and even had a fight scene. Anyone I've shown that DVD to still cracks up watching it, but I don't care. For me, it was proof that I could create something lasting. That little taste of acting didn't bring fame or money, but it gave me belief, belief that I could chase dreams on my own terms. If I could go from outsider to insider once, I could do it again. That thought kept me moving when nothing else did.

Still, outside of that, I was lost. The one thing I had going for me was a free apartment and a small paycheck for picking up trash and cleaning student housing. It wasn't glamorous, but it gave me time and space to think. Even then, I knew I couldn't float like that forever.

One afternoon, while helping a new resident move furniture upstairs, I noticed how jacked he was. Dude had veins popping out everywhere. I asked him what he did to get in such good shape, and he told me he boxed. I didn't think much of it until a month later, when he spotted me working out in the school gym and said, "You want a real workout? Come with me."

You don't get better by fighting easy fights.

That first workout nearly broke me, but I didn't quit. The guy who brought me noticed. Then Gus noticed. He told me if I kept showing up and putting in the work, I could become a good fighter. From that day forward, I was hooked. The gym became my new community, my new classroom. For the first time since high school, I wasn't just surviving a new environment; I had direction.

When I told friends and family I was starting to box, some laughed. Honestly, I couldn't blame them.

Around that time, I was trying to keep everything else in my life from falling apart. My father had bought me a 1990 Dodge Shadow from the junkyard. The ignition was shot, so I had to start it with a screwdriver. That worked fine until one day I got pulled over, and the cops assumed I'd stolen it. Once they saw the paperwork and realized how genuine I was, they let me go. That little Shadow wasn't much, but it took me everywhere, class, work, the gym, even the Texas State Fair. It wasn't pretty, but it gave me freedom. I didn't have much, but I had motion.

That car was kind of like me, beat up, patched together, but still running. Life will test whatever peace you think you've found, and before long, mine did. I started realizing I needed something steady, something bigger than myself. I began getting involved with a big local church in Plano. I didn't have money to give, so I tithed my time. Volunteering grounded me. It gave me faith when everything else felt uncertain. I needed something to believe in while I was trying to believe in myself.

Then came a lesson I'll never forget.

In 2005, my father was heading out of town, and I asked if I could borrow his 1994 Cadillac, the one everyone called the "Mack-alac." He said yes, but told me not to go anywhere except work and the gym because the tags were expired. What he didn't know was that I had a bunch of unpaid tickets from my old car.

So there I was at a QuikTrip, filling up the Cadillac when it happened. My foot slipped from the brake to the gas, and the car lurched forward, straight over the curb, into a water-bottle display, and almost through the wall. Police showed up, ran my name, and found a warrant for unpaid tickets. The officer was actually kind and even laughed when he found a "Get Out of Jail Free" card from Monopoly in my wallet.

The funny part ended fast, though. My Pops and Aunt San were both in Chicago, so no one could bail me out. I ended up spending two nights in jail before they even figured out where I was. When they finally did, they got the tickets cleared, and I walked out with one promise to myself: I was never going back. Sitting in that cell, I knew I'd pushed my luck too far.

That was the day I learned two things: pay your tickets, and get your own damn car.

I scraped together enough cash to buy a 1993 Plymouth Acclaim that looked like it was built from four or five different cars. It was every color of the rainbow and broke down every other day. I spent more time in junkyards than on the road, but it ran, most days. My friends knew that if their phone rang after dark, it was probably me stranded somewhere. I laughed it off, but it wore on me.

Once, I took a girl out on a date, and I'm pretty sure she said yes because she thought I was some elite boxer. That illusion disappeared fast when she saw my car. I didn't care, it ran, and that was enough.

When it didn't, I took the DART bus. I'd ride after long days of training, exhausted, sometimes falling asleep and missing my stop. Still, I showed up every single day. I learned to be grateful. Some people would've loved to have that broken-down car, and that kept me humble. I knew effort was the only thing I could control.

Through all of that, the busted cars, the late nights, the exhaustion, I kept showing up to the gym. Every day, I pushed through. After a few consistent weeks, Gus started taking notice. He saw something in me and decided to invest his time in training me.

Not long after, I fought my first amateur match, with Gus in my corner. For a guy who started boxing a decade later than most fighters, that first bout was everything. Gus gave me the confidence to believe I could actually compete. Still, not everyone shared his belief. Even my Pops laughed at the idea when I told him.

"Boy," he said, "you're gonna get your ass knocked out." He was joking when he said it. That was just Pops, but I took it seriously. Truth is, he supported everything I ever tried. He teased me, sure, but he always believed in me.

And honestly, he had every reason to think that. I'd only been training for a few months, and I had no experience. But I figured, what did I have to lose? Worst case, I could always mix boxing with acting and try to become a pro wrestler in the WWE. I wasn't scared of failing anymore, just standing still.

Three months later, I stepped into the ring for my first amateur fight. Even without a real sports background, I was pretty muscular, which put me in the super-heavyweight division. That meant I was fighting grown men with way more experience, guys who'd been boxing longer than I'd been alive.

It was a war. I had no skills, no rhythm, and no plan except to keep swinging. My opponent was thirty years old, built like a tank, and he knew what he was doing. But I held my ground. Neither of us got knocked out, but I came up short on the scorecards.

After the fight, Pops walked over with a grin.

"I got my ass kicked, Pops," I said.

He nodded and laughed, "Yeah, son, you got your ass kicked for sure."

I thought he'd be mad that I cursed, but he wasn't. He could see it, the heart. He knew I wasn't just playing around. That beating wasn't the end of something; it was the beginning. Losing didn't scare me anymore; quitting did.

I went back to the gym that Monday like nothing happened. Kept training. Kept fighting. I did a few more amateur smokers, little unsanctioned fights to gain experience. I won a few, lost a few, but never quit. Each one taught me something about patience, pacing, and how to think in the ring instead of just brawling. And then came my first real shot: the 2006 Golden Gloves tournament in Dallas.

Losing didn't scare me anymore; quitting did.

I entered the heavyweight novice division (178 to 201 pounds) and fought my way through every match until I won the championship. That first Golden Gloves title changed everything. It proved that all the sweat, all the busted cars, all the sleepless nights were leading somewhere. For the first time, I knew I wasn't imagining my potential.

After that, people started to know my name. Even when Gus's gym shut down, I knew I couldn't stop. That win showed me I belonged in the ring. I wasn't chasing an idea anymore. I was a fighter, on paper and in my spirit. But every fighter knows: the real challenge starts when the lights go off and the work begins again.

REFLECTIONS

WHEN YOU COMMIT, GIVE IT 110%

> *Half-effort won't save you. When life's on the line, give it everything and then some.*

It's worth repeating: boxing literally saved my life. I've always taken everything I do seriously, but it wasn't until a friend introduced me to the sport that I realized sometimes giving 100 percent still isn't enough. If it weren't for him, I wouldn't know this sport or the work ethic it taught me.

In training, 110 percent meant staying an extra hour after everyone left to work the bag. It meant sparring even when I was exhausted. It meant studying film of fighters I'd never heard of just to understand footwork and timing. That commitment, to give more than what's expected, more than what's comfortable, is what carried me through every fight since.

FIND YOUR PASSION

> *Once you find what lights you up, the rest of the world starts to make sense.*

I had never been an athlete. I sucked at everything I ever played, football, basketball, whatever it was. To this day, I'm not athletic unless it's boxing. But the second I stepped into the ring, something clicked. Everything that felt awkward everywhere else suddenly made sense. The rhythm, the timing, the discipline, it all fit me. Boxing showed me what passion feels like, and once I found it, I stopped doubting what I was built for.

ADDING VALUE IS GIVING, TOO

> *You don't need money to give back. Time, talent, and energy are gifts that multiply.*

It might sound easy when I talk about giving back, but it's hard for people working nonstop just to make ends meet. Not everyone has money or time to spare. Still, I've learned that value itself is a form of giving.

We all have something unique to offer, skills, insight, energy, empathy, and not all of it requires cash or calendar space. Sometimes giving back just means noticing what's needed and filling that gap. Whether it's encouragement, effort, or wisdom, generosity starts with awareness. That's a kind of wealth no paycheck can replace.

ACT LIKE YOU BELONG

> *Confidence creates opportunity. Walk into every room like your purpose already opened the door.*

One thing I learned early in my career was that nobody was going to hand me acceptance. I was always the late starter, the guy who began boxing after everyone else. My abilities were questioned, and people expected me to prove myself twice as hard. Instead of overthinking it, I focused on results. I knew what I wanted and moved with purpose. If you carry yourself like you belong, sooner or later, everyone else will see it too.

CORNER QUESTIONS

1. Where are you still giving half effort and expecting full results?

2. What would 110 percent look like for you right now?

3. Who helped you see your potential when you didn't see it yourself?

First real shots—where you learn fast if you love the fight.

Scorecards don't reward noise—they reward control.

Guard up—discipline when your body wants to panic.

Work behind the jab—effort that adds up round after round.

BETWEEN THE ROPES

"The ring doesn't lie, it shows you who you really are."

Champions aren't made by lights; they're built through repetition. The solitary work fortifies strengths that noise can't reach.

Every fighter faces a point when small wins aren't enough. For me, that point came after that first Golden Gloves run, when I realized I needed more than raw effort, I needed sharper tools. I competed in more matches, continually finding ways to succeed.

Around that time, I began searching for a new training spot when a friend told me about a gym in Garland run by a renowned trainer named Paul Vazquez. Paul was strictly old school, the kind of coach who lived and breathed boxing. He even had a full gym in his backyard, not some makeshift setup. His place was more upscale than many professional gyms I'd seen. I remember feeling like I'd stepped into a world I wasn't sure I deserved yet.

Paul taught a hard-nosed, disciplined style. He had so many fighters that it was understandable he didn't know all our names, mine included. But that didn't bother me. I kept showing up day after day, training like someone who had something to prove. Whenever there was a tournament, I was there. I wanted him to notice my work before he noticed my name.

By the time I really started winning, boxing wasn't a hobby anymore, it was my life. I'd been grinding through local tournaments, earning respect around Dallas, and learning what it truly meant to fight through exhaustion, doubt, and pain.

After one of those early tournament wins, Paul looked at me and said, "Where the hell did you come from?"

I just smiled and said, "I've been here the whole time."

Hearing that from him made every lonely drill worth it. From that day on, things changed between us. Paul took me on as his fighter and helped me reach the next level.

In 2007, at twenty-two, the Golden Gloves came around again, and I won, this time under Coach Paul. Once he brought me into his circle, everything got serious. Training wasn't something I did after class anymore; it was my day. I'd wake up sore, go to class, squeeze in a work shift, and still hit the gym every night. The other fighters started noticing I wasn't just showing up, I was chasing something. Every spar, every round, every drill was another test of how bad I wanted it. It felt like my whole life started orbiting around those rounds.

People started to know who I was. I wasn't just the new guy with potential anymore; I was the one to watch. And to think, I'd only started boxing at twenty, a late start by any standard. I wasn't a natural talent; boxing made me one. But once it did, I became obsessed. I studied fighters like Andre Ward, Sergio Martinez, Andre Berto, and Marvin Hagler, breaking down their fights like homework.

For my first few bouts, I didn't even know how to cut weight properly, which put me at a disadvantage against opponents who understood the science of the sport. Every mistake showed me how far I still had to go. Coach Paul believed in me anyway. He saw something raw and built on it. If it weren't for him, my boxing career might have taken a completely different turn.

Every boxer hits that point when the rounds get harder, when the gloves feel heavier, the air gets thinner, and it's no longer about talent. It's about grit. That's where I was. These were the rounds that tested what I was made of. Some nights I questioned if I had anything left, but quitting never crossed my mind. That belief, and that grind, started paying off when I defended that title in 2007, showing it wasn't luck. Each win gave me more than confidence; it gave me purpose.

Outside the ring, life didn't slow down. I was still fighting, just in different rounds. My love for boxing, combined with the flexibility of attending and working at Collin County Community College, allowed me to stay longer than most people would at a two-year school. Back then, the school wasn't yet known as the top-ranked community college in Texas like it is today, but I was starting to build a name on campus.

It was strange being respected in two different worlds at once. I became somewhat of a local celebrity, one of the first students ever considered for a U.S. Olympic team, with multiple tournament wins under my belt. But here's the truth: boxing didn't pay. It actually cost money. Between training, eating right, and traveling for fights, I was constantly broke. My education and my boxing were linked; if one stopped, so did the other. That wasn't an option.

So I hustled. Books, food, gas, travel, I had to find ways to cover it all. I juggled classes, training, and a handful of side jobs to keep myself afloat. One of those jobs was at the student housing complex, doing maintenance and cleanup. That's where I met Cal.

We were both broke, but determined not to stay that way. Cal was fast-talking, sharp, always on the move, another young hustler who refused to sit still. We clicked immediately because we shared that grind mentality. One day, he saw the boxing trophies on my desk and started asking about my fights. I mentioned I had a Golden Gloves tournament coming up that weekend. He said he'd come watch. I didn't think much of it, people say that all the time, but sure enough, I looked out after the fight and there he was, camera in hand, cheering me on. Having someone show up for me like that hit different.

Cal later told me there was something about my positivity that was contagious. I think that's what connected us; we both believed in possibility, even when we had nothing.

Cal was always hustling to make money, so when he pitched an idea to throw a party at his barber's shop, I was in. It sounded wild, but we both had that "why not?" attitude.

In early 2007, Justin Timberlake was performing at the American Airlines Center, and we decided to use that concert crowd to promote our party. We spent hours walking the parking lot, sliding flyers on cars, handing them out to anyone who'd take one. Eventually, we crossed the street to the W Hotel, a hotspot for celebrities back then. I was nervous, but acting confident had become a skill by then.

We had no business being there, but that never stopped us. We sat at the bar acting like we belonged, even though we barely had money for drinks. Then I realized the woman sitting next to me was Gabrielle Union.

I looked over and, without missing a beat, asked if I could buy her a drink. She said yes.

Now, nothing came of it, but that one "yes" reminded me that confidence opens doors. Later that night, we somehow made it upstairs to the Ghost Bar, one of the most exclusive lounges in Dallas. We were suddenly surrounded by pro athletes, artists, and people we'd only seen on TV. And instead of feeling out of place, we acted like we were supposed to be there.

Those moments showed me something powerful: belonging isn't granted, it's claimed.

When the night of our party finally came, it was a madhouse. Over three hundred people showed up, cars lined the block, and the shop was packed wall to wall. Cal flew in friends from New York to bartend, and my Pops even helped with security. Since we couldn't legally sell alcohol, we sold "tickets" that included drinks. It wasn't exactly by the book, but it worked. We made a solid profit and got a real taste of entrepreneurship. For the first time, I felt like I could build something outside the ring.

That night gave me confidence. It taught me that with enough hustle, you can create your own opportunities. But it also reminded me where my real peace was, the quiet hum of the gym lights and the rhythm of gloves hitting the bag.

People used to think I was soft because I smiled a lot and never acted like a tough guy. They didn't realize how serious I was about boxing until they stepped into the ring with me, and then they learned quick. My actions spoke louder than any attitude could.

That night reminded me why I couldn't stop boxing. It wasn't just about titles, it was about survival.

Boxing gave me purpose and respect, but humility kept me grounded.

I still remember the last time I went back to Pleasant Grove. I was in college and wanted to pick up some of the guys for a party. None of them had cars, so I drove down to get Pooh and the crew.

The second I walked into that house, it was like stepping into a movie scene, or a nightmare. Everyone had masks on, shirts off, guns out, drugs on the table. I remember standing there thinking, this is not where I belong anymore. I couldn't get out of there fast enough. It scared me how quickly my life could've snapped back into the old one.

Even now, I think about how easily things could've gone wrong in that moment. If cops had raided the place, or if a robbery had gone down, I would've been just another bystander in the wrong place at the wrong time. Dead or in jail, it would've been the same outcome.

I didn't have much money back then, and what little I earned went to tuition, food, and boxing. To make ends meet, I took every odd job I could find around campus. That maintenance gig at the apartments gave me free rent and a sense of independence. I used to joke that I was a "sanitation engineer," but really, I didn't care what I did as long as it moved me toward my goals. Survival made you creative if you wanted something bad enough.

That season of my life, balancing school, work, and the ring, built a kind of discipline I hadn't known before. When I brought that focus back to boxing, everything started clicking.

By late 2008, I had ten novice fights under my belt and had to make a decision: stay comfortable or move up to "big boy open." Once you go open, there's no hiding. You can face anyone, from Olympians to national champions. So I waited a bit, stacking more experience before making the jump.

When I finally did, my first open fight was at the Dallas Golden Gloves, the regional tournament that leads to the Texas State Championships. My bracket didn't have a first-round opponent, so I advanced straight to round two, and my draw was brutal.

I got matched with Craig Baker from Houston, the reigning national champion. He was ranked number three in the country and had hundreds of amateur fights under his belt. I'd be lying if I said I wasn't scared, but I was also fired up. I wanted to test myself against the best. Walking toward that ring felt like walking toward the truth.

Craig beat me. Clean. No excuses. But I fought with everything I had, and even in losing, I grew.

Later that same year, USA Boxing held a qualifying tournament for the 2008 Olympic Trials. Once again, I advanced automatically in the first round, no opponent in my bracket, and once again, I drew Craig Baker in the next round. This time, the fight was closer. I'd learned, adjusted, and stood my ground. Still, he edged me out and ended my run. Losing twice to the same man pushed me harder than any win ever had.

The Olympics wasn't my destination, it was my training ground.

But something changed in those losses. It's like I picked up part of his skill, his rhythm, his calm. I came out of those fights sharper, hungrier, and ready to dominate.

By 2009, Craig had turned pro, and the path cleared. I entered the Dallas Golden Gloves and cleaned house. Then I went to the Texas State Golden Gloves—Houston, San Antonio, El Paso—it didn't matter who stood across from me. I ran through everyone and took the state title at 201 pounds, earning my spot on the Dallas team heading to nationals.

In May 2009, I represented Texas at the National Golden Gloves in Utah. My first fight was against the St. Louis champion, and it was a war. I thought I'd done enough to win, but the judges saw it differently.

Losing stung, but it fueled me. I walked out of that ring knowing I was close, closer than ever.

A month later, the USA Boxing Tournament came around in Denver. I didn't have money to go, but Coach Paul and a friend drove me there themselves. That's love you never forget.

Nationals was my breakout. I beat the Navy champ. Then Hawaii's champ. Then the Kansas City champion, ranked #3 in the nation at the time. I made it all the way to the semifinals, where I faced Jordan Shimmell, and that's where my run ended.

Jordan beat me and went on to win the whole tournament, but finishing in the top four earned me a spot on the USA Team. When I saw that "Welcome to Team USA" packet in my mailbox, I knew I'd made it. I was now ranked third in the nation. Holding that packet felt like holding proof that every sacrifice mattered.

Each morning at training camp in Colorado Springs, I'd wake up, look out the window, and see Olympians in every sport, wrestlers, gymnasts, fencers, all grinding. It was humbling and inspiring. I trained under Barry Hunter, one of the best, and ate in the same cafeteria as national champions.

They warned us about the food being loaded with fiber, but I didn't listen. Let's just say the aftermath was rough. Still, every bit of it felt worth it.

In October 2009, I fought my first international match against Wadi Camacho of Great Britain. Their team was stacked; Anthony Joshua was on it. Wadi wasn't Joshua, but he was big and skilled. I fought hard, but he beat me. I was a smaller heavyweight, so after that, I started cutting down to 178 to stay competitive. Losing overseas hit different; it made me hungry to prove I belonged on any stage.

Then came the World Series of Boxing, WSB, a league where elite amateurs fought without headgear and still kept amateur status. I got drafted by the Memphis Force and loved every minute of it. The wildest part? My ring entrance was announced by Andre Ward himself, one of my idols. Hearing him call my name and mention my goals, training fighters, opening a gym, was surreal.

Eventually, USA Boxing decided WSB fighters could still compete for the Olympics, and I entered the 2011 Olympic Trials. I lost to Jerry Odom, one of the best in the division. It hurt. I believed I'd won, but the judges didn't. Even so, that fight earned me respect from everyone who watched. Losses like that stay with you in ways wins never do.

Then came the final shot, the "Last Chance" qualifier in Mobile, Alabama. I was twenty-seven, and my first-round opponent was my friend Robert Brant. Cutting to 178 put us in the same bracket, and one of us had to go home.

When the bell rang, friendship disappeared. Robert was slick, Mayweather-style. I was the pressure fighter. We went back and forth until the bell, and when they announced the score, he'd beaten me by thirteen points. My Olympic dream was over. Hearing that score felt like someone pressed pause on everything.

I could've been bitter, but I wasn't. That fight lit the fuse for what came next. I didn't know it yet, but losing that Olympic shot was winning something bigger: my purpose outside the ring. It was the end of one chapter and the start of the next.

REFLECTIONS

POINT A TO POINT B

> *Help shows up for those already moving. Start pushing and watch how fast support appears.*

No one's coming to carry you where you want to go. That's just life. Opportunities show up when you're already moving, not when you're standing still. I always think about something Chris Rock once said about having a flat tire: if you're just standing there waiting for help, nobody stops, but when you start pushing the car yourself, people pull over to help. That stuck with me. Help shows up for people who help themselves. That's been my story from day one: get moving, and the right people appear.

MASTER YOUR CRAFT

> *Consistency beats talent. Keep sharpening your tools until skill feels like instinct.*

Hard work alone isn't enough, only intentional work compounds. I learned that through film study, footwork, pace control, and perfecting the right jab for the right moment. Sweat turned into skill because I practiced exactly what I'd need under lights, not what just felt good in the gym.

Business works the same way. The goal isn't perfection; it's precision. At my gym now, I teach fighters the same principle: refine the repeatable, measure results, and stay curious. Mastery isn't a finish line, it's a mindset. Show up, tighten one screw every day, and before long, you've built something unstoppable.

UNDERSTAND WHAT MAKES YOU TICK

> *Know your wiring and work with it. Self-awareness turns struggle into strategy.*

Just because you explain something to me doesn't mean I'll automatically get it. I need to hear things in usable terms, how to apply them, not just what they mean. Once I understand the why, it sticks. That's how I learn best, and over time I realized that was one of my superpowers.

That mindset shaped how I train others. In boxing, every move has purpose, each punch sets up the next, like chess. Teaching fighters the "why" behind their choices gives them control. It's the same outside the ring. Understanding people means seeing what motivates them. If I hadn't struggled the way I did growing up, I wouldn't connect as deeply with others today. What once felt like a weakness turned into my biggest strength.

ALWAYS FIND A WAY

> *Obstacles test creativity. Where resources fall short, grit bridges the gap.*

When resources were scarce, relationships carried me. Coach Paul drove me to Denver when I had no money for nationals. A friend let me use his car when mine broke down for the third time that month. Another gym let me train for free when I couldn't afford dues. Those weren't lucky breaks, they were returns on the respect and effort I'd invested in people.

Finding a way doesn't mean scrambling; it means staying ready. When you prepare fully, even a cracked-open door becomes an opportunity. Resourcefulness is a mix of humility and hustle: ask for help, show gratitude, and prove through your consistency that you're worth betting on.

MENTORS EVOLVE WITH YOUR JOURNEY

> *Every level needs a new teacher. The right guide shows up when you're ready to grow.*

No matter what you're chasing, it helps to have someone you trust showing you the ropes. In boxing, that's especially true because the risks are real. When I first walked into a gym, it wasn't anything fancy, just a storefront with a ring and a bunch of hungry fighters. But that's where I found belonging and discipline.

Gus Samuelson taught me the basics. Paul Vazquez refined my technique and pushed me to the national level. Barry Hunter at Team USA taught me to think like a chess player. Each mentor prepared me for the next stage. The right mentors don't just train your body; they shape your mindset. And as you grow, your teachers change. Every level requires new guidance, but the same lesson remains: stay teachable, and the right people will always show up when you're ready.

BY ANY MEANS NECESSARY

> *If the goal is worthy, hustle until it happens. Creativity turns "can't afford it" into "already done."*

My trainers and coaches were incredible, they helped with travel expenses and trained me for less than they were worth. But I knew that was too big a burden to put on them. So we came up with the idea of a fundraiser. I can't even swear it was all my idea, but my Aunt San embraced it with open arms. She let me use her house and cooked everything. All I had to do was put out the word, and I texted every single person in my phone.

That's how we made it happen. No excuses. If the goal is worthy, you hustle until it's real. Family stepped up, friends stepped in, and the community carried the rest. Creativity turned "can't afford it" into "already done."

CORNER QUESTIONS

1. What discipline are you building when no one's watching?

2. Are you practicing consistency or just activity?

3. What "gym" in your life do you keep avoiding because it exposes your weaknesses?

Me and Coach Vazquez in the early days—he saw something in me long before I saw it in myself.

Coach Vazquez in my corner—steady, sharp, and believing in me every time I stepped into the ring.

Cal and me—broke, hungry, and learning how to create opportunities.

Tournament wins—proof the work was paying off.

CHANGING CORNERS

"Growth means knowing when to switch corners, and who's in them."

Anyone can swing hard in the first round. True fighters learn how to breathe through the late ones. I was starting to feel those late rounds in my real life, too.

By 2011, I was still chasing the Olympic dream, but this time I was doing it on my own terms at F2L Gym, the place where I worked to pay for every mile of that journey. I wasn't getting rich, but I was earning every inch.

Around that time, my boy Calvin went on to intern with Def Jam Records. Through that opportunity, he started getting invited to high-profile industry parties alongside DJ Kid Capri, YG, and Jeremih. Sometimes he'd call me up and say, "TMACK, you gotta roll with me." I'd show up, and every time he introduced me it was, "This is my friend, the boxer." There was something about that title that made me want to train even harder. Hearing it out loud made me feel like I had something to live up to. I couldn't let him have a friend who was a losing fighter. If you want to hang with the best, you've got to be the best. That's where the confidence to act like you belong really took hold for me. It wasn't about faking it; it was about preparing until you actually did belong.

The guy running the gym, we'll call him BT, was charismatic if nothing else. After the World Series of Boxing, we became good friends and even roomed together with a guy whom we just called "B," another fighter.

But charisma only gets you so far.

BT was a good friend to me, but he wasn't a good business partner. In business, he was inconsistent—missing sessions, dodging responsibilities, and always having a new excuse. I was already teaching boxing-fitness classes there for extra money, but that quickly turned into me covering his private lessons when he didn't show up. When payday came around, he'd have all the excuses in the world about why he didn't have the money to pay me. I kept swallowing my frustration because I needed the gym more than the argument.

Loyalty doesn't pay the bills, and consistency beats talk every single time.

He was one of the most loyal dudes on the street, but the opposite in the office. Still, I kept showing up because I believed in the dream. That gym was where I was building my name, my clientele, and my reputation. I didn't realize it then, but BT was teaching me a hard lesson about the business side of boxing: loyalty doesn't pay the bills, and consistency beats talk every single time.

Thankfully, fate stepped in. Through BT, I met a guy named Nate, someone who would change my life forever.

BT asked me to cover a class at Ringside Boxing one day, and Nate happened to be in it. We didn't know each other then, but we clicked right away. A year or so later, after I got back from the World Series of Boxing, BT lined up a job unloading blinds at Nate's warehouse. BT no-showed, so it ended up being just me and Nate unloading an entire truck by ourselves. Working beside him that day felt easy in a way I wasn't used to.

That day, we got to talking. He saw how hard I worked. I saw how honest and genuine he was. I didn't have a manager at the time, but when a contract from Prize Fight Promotions hit my inbox, Nate sat down with me, read it word for word, and broke it down line by line. That's when I asked him to be my boxing manager. From that point on, Nate had my back, in and out of the ring. Having someone explain things without judging me meant more than I ever let on.

Nate was the first person who really took a chance on me. I saw someone who'd already reached a level I was striving for; someone I could learn from. When I needed a job in college, he hired me. When I needed money to train or get to fights, he made sure I had it. When my car broke down for good, he helped me buy a new one. I paid him back, eventually, but without Nate, I would've been another statistic among boxers who never made it anywhere.

We came from two completely different worlds. Nate grew up in the Amish country of Lancaster, Pennsylvania. I grew up in Dallas. He had both parents at home; I was raised in a storm of chaos and change. But none of that stopped us from connecting. I never realized he went to a high school with only one Black kid, while I was that token Black kid in a mostly White school. He had to learn empathy. I had to learn trust. Somehow, our stories met right in the middle. It felt crazy how two opposite lives could line up at the right time.

BT kept being BT. Nate and I started to see the pattern. We realized he was trying to get away with things for as long as I'd let him. So we made a decision: it was time to push him out of the business. I knew it was coming, but saying it out loud still made my stomach drop.

That wasn't easy. I didn't like confrontation, but I was tired of being taken advantage of. The moment I stood my ground and said "no more," something shifted inside me. That's the day I stopped being just a fighter and started thinking like a professional.

That's when my Pops' old friend stepped in, a guy we all called "Champ." He was an old-school Dallas boxer, part hustler, part street legend, the kind of guy everyone in that world knew. My dad vouched for him because Champ had once been a serious fighter who'd gone toe-to-toe with some real names. I figured if Pops trusted him, I could too.

I started training at his gym because it was one of the nicest around, and honestly, I was looking for a fresh start away from BT's drama. At first, things were good. But then BT got in his ear about Nate, told him Nate was some rich White guy backing me, and that's when Champ flipped the switch. I could feel the energy shift before he even said a word.

He tried to hustle us. Told me my training would cost ten thousand dollars a month. I couldn't believe it. I didn't have that kind of money, and I sure wasn't about to let Nate get hustled, either. Nate was ready to help, but I said no. We weren't paying that.

That was another lesson right there, people will always test how much you believe in yourself. They'll see what they can get out of you if you let them. But the moment you stand up and say no, they lose their power. It felt good to finally trust my own judgment.

At that point, I was still hustling just to stay in the game. I didn't know my true worth. I was teaching personal-training sessions for $25 to $35 an hour, which I now realize was nothing compared to what my time was worth. But back then, it wasn't about money; it was about survival.

The cost of chasing the Olympic dream was steep, so Nate and my people put together a fundraiser to get me there. That support is the only reason I was able to keep going. Airfare, lodging, food, everything added up. I was barely making enough to cover my day-to-day bills, let alone travel for tournaments. That's when Nate stepped in again and helped me organize it.

We didn't have an official donation amount or a marketing plan. The message was simple: I had earned the opportunity to compete for the Olympic team, but the only thing holding me back was money. Nate started spreading the word, telling people how talented I was, and before long the buzz started to build.

When the day of the event came, I couldn't believe the turnout. It wasn't just family and friends; all my boxing clients from F2L showed up. Even Billy Brant, another trainer there who specialized in speed and agility, came through with his clients. The place was packed. Seeing that many people show up for me didn't feel real at first.

Everyone who knew me gave a speech, sharing how much it meant for me to chase that Olympic dream and thanking everyone for showing up. It was so humbling that I almost forgot the point was to raise money. But by the end of the night, we'd raised over $5,000, enough to keep me training, traveling, and fighting without being a burden on anyone else.

That night was special. It wasn't about the money, it was about community. It reminded me that people really believed in me, and that belief carried me through the disappointments that came later. I held onto that feeling every time things got rough.

But here's the thing, training with Champ quickly became another situation where I had to dig deep and say no. When he tried to hustle Nate for crazy sums of money to train me, Nate was actually considering it. But I wasn't having it. I knew Champ wasn't worth anywhere near what he wanted, and saying no to that hustle turned out to be the best decision I could've made. I'd learned the hard way that not every "coach" is a leader.

That "no" was the hardest and best decision I made.

That "no" led me straight to Derrick James, a move that changed everything.

While I was fighting in the amateurs, there was one guy I always paid attention to: Errol Spence Jr. Back then, he had that hard pressure style—always coming forward, always making you fight—like the Mexican-style pressure you see from certain camps. It wasn't about race. It was about rhythm.

And then his whole skill set transformed. He wasn't just brawling anymore—he was boxing beautifully. That's when we learned he'd been working with Derrick James. It wasn't a big headline at the time, but the results were obvious. Watching Errol level up told me Derrick knew something the rest of us didn't.

I already knew Derrick from my earlier boxing days. He used to be one of my sparring partners before he hung up the gloves. He would whoop my ass good in those sessions, but he always took time to explain why. Those explanations stuck with me more than the punches did.

When Nate and I realized Derrick was the one behind Errol's transformation, we approached him about training me. He agreed, and from that moment, everything started to come together. With Derrick in my corner, I knew I had what it took to make a real run at turning professional.

The right corner can change the whole fight.

That event, the fundraiser, the setbacks, the hustles, the people who believed in me, it all came together to teach me one big lesson: support doesn't always come from where you expect it. Sometimes it's not even about the people you lose, it's about the people you gain along the way. The right corner can change the whole fight.

With Derrick James in my corner, I knew I had everything I needed to make a real run at going professional. After all the false starts, hustles, and lessons, it finally felt like every round I'd ever fought, inside and outside the ring, had led to this moment. The bell was about to ring on an entirely new fight: the one that would test everything I'd learned so far. I could feel the next chapter pulling me forward.

REFLECTIONS

STAY HUMBLE

> *Victory means nothing if ego takes over. Remember who you were before the lights came on.*

Growing up the way I did, I was never conceited. I didn't have much to brag about. Even when I won things I never imagined, Class President, Homecoming King, I didn't let it change me. I enjoyed the moment and kept moving.

That carried into college. I could win the best fight of my life and be right back the next morning picking up trash or moving furniture just to keep my dreams alive. But humility gets tested when the stage gets bigger. Small venues are easy to stay grounded in. Big arenas are different. When thousands are watching and your name is in lights, it hits you like electricity.

I didn't see it then, but my trainers did. They reminded me to stay focused and humble. It didn't matter who showed up or how bright the lights were. What mattered was staying the same Tony from sparring, giving everything I had.

SAY NO TO HEAR YES

> *The right no clears the path for the yes you were built for.*

For most of my life, my philosophy was to say "yes" to as many things as possible, especially to life itself. But with time, I learned that sometimes the most powerful move you can make is saying no.

We all have limited time and energy, and the things we give up often define our path as much as what we choose. The sacrifice makes success meaningful. The anticipation, doubt, and perseverance that come from turning down something tempting in the moment build the discipline needed to reach your real goal.

Saying no to BT's broken promises and Champ's hustle opened space for Derrick James, the yes I was meant for. Boundaries don't close doors; they clear your path.

STAY ON YOUR JAB

> *Keep your rhythm, keep your focus. Life hits hard, your attitude is the defense that wins rounds.*

The jab is the most important punch in boxing. It's not flashy or the shot that ends a fight, but it's the foundation. A jab can be offense or defense. If you're on the ropes, a few jabs create space. If you're hurt, the jab keeps your opponent back. When you're attacking, it sets up the knockout. It's the most thrown punch for a reason, and it means more than people realize.

The jab is your attitude in life. Staying on your jab helps you handle the good and recover from the bad. When things go wrong, don't panic, stay steady. When things go right, don't rush, stay sharp.

My positive outlook has always been my jab. A smile opens doors and sets the tone. I treat everyone with equal respect, no pedestals, no shortcuts. I tell my fighters the same: mistakes can be fixed, but a negative mindset will beat you first.

MINDSET

> *Winners think different. Vision, belief, and confidence can out-punch any advantage.*

When I walked into Derrick's gym, I didn't just need better technique, I needed to believe I belonged at the next level. That shift in mindset, from "I'm trying to make it" to "I'm ready to compete with anyone," is what changed everything.

Confidence without competence is delusion. But competence without confidence is wasted potential. The fighters who make it aren't always the most talented, they're the ones who believe they belong before anyone tells them they do. I learned that lesson at those industry parties with Cal, and I applied it in the ring. Asking questions without fear, walking into rooms like I earned my spot, and trusting my preparation, that opened more doors than talent ever could.

CORNER QUESTIONS

1. What keeps you going when the crowd stops cheering?

2. When have you mistaken pride for perseverance?

3. Who in your corner right now is there out of loyalty, and who's there because they're making you better?

With my team, Derrick James, Nate, and Robert, in the locker room before a major fight.

Representing Team USA—early amateur days when repetition, discipline, and belief turned a late starter into a real contender.

The squad—iron sharpening iron, round after round.

The team—the people who pushed me, sharpened me, and made me better.

FIGHT TO FINISH

"Your mind will quit before your body does."

The toughest lesson in fighting isn't just throwing punches—it's figuring out who really belongs in your corner. I learned that watching film. One coach could watch a round and point out everything I did wrong. Nate would watch the same tape and show me what was working, then tell me how to build on it. Same footage. Two completely different messages. That shift hit me harder than most punches, and it didn't just make me a better fighter—it changed how I coach and how I lead.

As I've already mentioned, I started boxing at twenty, which is about as late as someone can bloom in the sport and still have the hope of making it professional. I never even had an athletic bone in my body until boxing clicked for me. But I quickly became a student of the sport, watching the matches of guys like Andre Ward, Sergio Martinez, Andre Berto, and Marvin Hagler. For my first few fights, I had no idea how to cut weight the right way, which put me at a disadvantage against opponents who were in better shape because they knew the mechanics and science better than I did. Even now that my career in the ring is over, I find myself becoming more disciplined every day. I knew nothing about business when I opened my gym. If I compare myself to other business owners with similar annual revenues, I probably know less "by the book" than most of them, and I'm okay with that, because it keeps me hungry and willing to learn. I've always learned by messing up first and figuring it out on the way.

I would have missed out on so much if I hadn't learned to say no to the two trainers who came before Derrick. Each decision, each "no," hardened me for what was coming next, the years of sweat, sacrifice, and scorecards that would define the rest of my career. I also look back on the fighters who were part of that year's tournament and am humbled by making it as far as I did. Errol Spence Jr., who I mentioned earlier, was on the team along with several other guys I always looked up to. Knowing I belonged in that lineup still surprises me sometimes.

With Nate's help in securing Derrick James as my new trainer, I began training at the Cooper Institute, where Derrick worked. That place was a blessing, cutting-edge facilities, elite athletes, and even former presidents trained there. I still remember crossing paths with George W. Bush one morning and getting a picture with him. For a kid from Dallas who once struggled just to find gym time, it was surreal. Moments like that reminded me how far I'd come without even noticing it in real time.

Some of my early experiences with Derrick, along with the words of wisdom he shared with me over the years, have stayed with me to this day and shaped how I coach my own clients. The way Derrick was used to training fighters didn't resonate with me at first. He could have kept forcing his approach or walked away, but instead he chose to adapt. Derrick wanted to see me succeed, so he adjusted to my style of learning, which made all the difference, because I just couldn't seem to grasp the lessons to save my life. On the rare occasions I did, I couldn't retain them for long. I'd go home beating myself up, wondering if the problem was in my body or in my head. It was the first time I realized how much patience it takes to believe in someone who's still trying to believe in himself.

I think this experience was as impactful for Derrick as it was for me. He was used to coaching world champions who understood instantly, and I was the first fighter who didn't. But he knew I wasn't unique; if someone with my drive could struggle like that, others would too. I always remember him telling me, "I'm not going to quit on you, Tony. I'm going to go further than far."

"I'm not going to quit on you, Tony. I'm going to go further than far."

Once Derrick changed his approach with me, everything started falling into place. One of my biggest flaws was being a perfectionist. I was so focused on nailing everything 100 percent that I forgot how to enjoy the process. You have to remember why you started and why you love it, or your body and mind will fight you every step of the way. When you love what you're doing, you grow faster. Even then, you never really master it just because you got it right once. I had to teach myself to breathe, not brace, every time something felt hard.

As my boxing career climbed to higher levels, Derrick helped keep me grounded. He taught me focus and humility in the ring, lessons that still guide me in life and business. When you're in there fighting for your life, adrenaline takes over, and it's easy to celebrate, to showboat, to throw your hands up. But Derrick drilled it into me that winning itself is the celebration. If you step into every fight believing you can't lose, there's no need to act surprised when you don't.

Then came the sparring sessions that would sharpen me more than any fight ever could. Derrick had me sparring with Errol Spence Jr. as many as three times a week. Errol was already achieving what I dreamed of, and those sessions forced me to rise to that level. Thanks to Derrick and those grueling rounds, I not only turned professional but finished my career with a 13-1-1 record and the Texas Super Middleweight Championship title. Those rounds with Errol made me grow up fast.

Derrick even helped me financially, just like Coach Paul once had. He knew I couldn't afford a full-time coach's rate, so he trained me for less than he was worth and waited until I got paid to collect his cut. That kind of loyalty sticks with you.

Our relationship was great for about three years, but as Derrick's reputation exploded and world champions began lining up for his time, I started feeling the distance. Around that same time, Derrick began working with Jermell Charlo, and I could feel his schedule—and priorities—shifting fast.

He was spending more time with guys like Errol, who were progressing faster, and I could tell I wasn't a priority anymore. Eventually, he told Nate he no longer had time to train me. I respected it, but it hurt. Still, that's the fight game. Losing a corner man feels a lot like losing a round you thought you won.

Not long after, I ran into my first real lesson in the professional world of boxing outside the gym. One of my early promoters had me fooled for a while. He was funny, charismatic, and seemed to know everyone. I didn't realize his reputation for being one of the shadiest characters in the business until it was too late. Looking back, I should've trusted that uneasy feeling in my gut.

At first, he impressed me because he kept finding fights, sometimes on short notice, always with decent payouts. Later on, I learned he was playing both sides of the business in a way that put his fighters at risk. He'd hype us up while quietly stacking the odds the other direction. If Nate hadn't started digging into opponents and situations, my career might've ended a lot sooner.

This promoter loved to stroke my ego. He'd tell me how weak my opponents were, how they had no power, how they stood no chance against me. But Nate started researching them on YouTube, and what he found was the exact opposite. The guy who "couldn't punch" was knocking people out cold. The one who "wasn't fast" was dancing circles around his opponents. That promoter wanted me overconfident because he was likely betting against me. It was wild realizing someone smiling in your face could be hoping you fall.

It was a hard truth to swallow, but it became another valuable lesson, never hand control of your career to someone who benefits more when you lose than when you win.

I still blame that promoter for the only loss on my record. It was August 2013, and he set me up to fight Lee Campbell, one of those "no-power" guys. The fight was scheduled for only six rounds, shorter than the bouts I was used to. I dropped the first couple of rounds trying to adjust to his awkward style, then found my rhythm and took it the distance. The judges scored it a majority decision for him, two for Campbell, one a draw. Walking back to the locker room, I felt the weight of everyone else's choices on my shoulders.

Sometimes you have to lose sight to truly see.

It stung, but knowing the situation wasn't built for me to win gave me perspective. Even when people don't believe in you, or when they're just protecting their own interests, you can still show up, fight hard, and make sure no setback defines you.

After the Campbell fight, my career was still climbing. I was getting better, smarter, and hungrier. But life had other plans.

A few weeks before my second-to-last fight, scheduled against Marcus Upshaw, officials sent me for a routine eye exam. The optometrist noticed something strange but didn't have the right tools to confirm it. I was referred to a retina specialist, who also saw cause for concern. I wasn't about to let them cancel my fight, so I made sure to talk it through, explaining how important it was. They thought it might be a cataract, something minor, and cleared me. I kept telling myself it was nothing, hoping my body would listen.

That fight with Upshaw was a war. It went the distance, both of us battered but unbroken, and it ended in a draw. That was April 2015. My next fight, in June 2015, was against Joshua Robertson, and it turned out to be my last. I won by first-round TKO, and for a moment, everything felt perfect.

That was early summer 2015. Not long after, my world had started to blur, literally.

A few weeks later, I was hanging out at Robert Brant's house with his wife, shooting a pellet gun at soda cans like we'd done a hundred times before. I couldn't hit the target to save my life. Every time I squinted, it felt like something was blocking my vision. I laughed it off, but deep down I knew something was wrong. It scared me in a way I didn't want to say out loud yet.

A week later, I was back in the gym sparring Tobius Sims, a guy I normally handled easily. This time, he kept tagging me with punches I never saw coming. A white curtain started closing over my eye. I told Nate, and he insisted we see a doctor right away.

The closest place open was the eye clinic inside a Walmart. That's where they told me my retina was detaching. They couldn't handle it there, so they sent me straight to Parkland Hospital, the same hospital in Dallas where I was born. Doctors said if they didn't operate immediately, I'd lose the eye. Hearing that felt like the floor dropped out from under me.

I had emergency surgery that night, and more surgeries followed in the months ahead. Just like that, my boxing career was gone. Winning by first-round TKO felt perfect, right up until life hit me with a punch I never saw coming.

I couldn't see punches coming anymore, but I started seeing life differently. The discipline that once kept me in the ring now kept my business and my purpose alive. Every surgery, every setback, every "no" along the way became proof of who I was without the gloves. Losing the fight game forced me to fight for myself in a new way.

Boxing built me, but losing it showed me what I was really fighting for. Sometimes you have to lose sight to truly see.

Having great trainers helped me get there faster, but no trainer in the world can teach toughness or heart. They can show you where to find it, but they can't give it to you. The most talented athlete on the planet, without the will to push past their limits, will never become great.

Some fighters care more about their records than the love of the sport. They protect their zero instead of defending their pride, taking easy fights and chasing payouts. That's never been me.

When I was 3–0, I fought a guy who was 6–0. When I was 7–0, I risked it against someone 5–0. I lost that one, but then won the next seven straight, most by knockout. I fought anyone they put in front of me because I wanted to be tested. I never wanted the easy road, I wanted the road that proved something.

That same mindset carried me from my first amateur bout to my final pro fight. No matter how many times I've been hit, cut, counted out, or overlooked, one truth never changed: I never stop fighting. Even when the ring was gone, that fight stayed in me.

REFLECTIONS

GUARD YOUR CIRCLE

> *Stay alert in business and life.*
> *Not everyone in your corner wants you to win.*

Starting a business was intimidating. I didn't have formal training, just what I learned watching my Pops and aunts work for themselves. I'd always been good at connecting with people, but creating value from nothing is a different challenge.

Boxing is a one-man sport, and that mindset shaped how I entered business. Boxing's back end taught me the biggest lesson: protect your inner circle. Some people I trusted cared more about their own money or reputation than my wins.

I push collaboration in Black communities, pool resources, build together, and see each other as teammates, not competition. Working with people like Derrick James and Amari Cooper showed me what real partnership looks like, and I'm committed to building more of that. I learned quick, loyalty without limits will get you knocked out. Every friend in the corner isn't your corner man.

TOMORROW IS PROMISED TO NO ONE

> *Every moment matters.*
> *Train, love, and live like the bell could ring at any second.*

When I started winning, I got swept up in the excitement. Going from never boxing to national tournaments that fast gave me an adrenaline rush and a confidence I'd never had. I kept chasing the next fight, the next chance to prove myself. Eventually I realized boxing could be my profession. I was holding my own with big names, and there was no reason to think I couldn't reach what they had.

No athlete wants to imagine it all ending, but it can. In boxing especially, admitting weakness feels unnatural. We're in a sport built on getting punched, cut, and bruised. If we stopped every time our hands hurt or our eye swelled, we'd be in the wrong business. But even warriors have limits.

Tomorrow isn't promised, and that truth changed how I trained, how I loved, and how I approached whatever rounds I had left.

SHOW ME THE ROPES

> *Seek wisdom, not shortcuts.*
> *The right mentor teaches you how to last, not just how to win.*

Whether you're an active fighter or running any business, you need managers you trust who align with your vision. My first manager was Nate, back when there wasn't much to manage. I was new, needed help with contracts, and had nowhere else to turn. Nate always had my best interest at heart, even when I couldn't pay him.

He also introduced me to his pastor, Keith Craft, which pushed me to take the business side seriously and get a coach with real industry experience. That's how I learned to last: not just by swinging harder, but by surrounding myself with people who wanted me to win the right way.

IT'S NO ACCIDENT

> *Success is built, not granted. Effort and faith make "luck" look inevitable.*

From the outside it might look like things came easily, great people in my corner, a level of success few reach. But none of it was an accident. When you put in the effort and do everything you're supposed to, and then some, God will get you where you're meant to go.

From day one I treated boxing like a job, not a hobby. Whether I had a fight coming up or not, you'd find me in the gym twice a day. Some people work out twice a week and convince themselves they're grinding. I lived there. Consistency and faith made what people call "luck" look inevitable.

FOCUS ON THE PROMISE, NOT THE PROBLEM

> *Shift your eyes from fear to faith.*
> *God's promise is bigger than any obstacle.*

Another principle I live by: most people focus on the problem; I focus on the promise. During one of my hardest seasons, a Joel Osteen sermon pushed me to open my Bible and look for what God actually said He would do. The more I studied His promises, the stronger my faith became.

We always have a choice: positive or negative, promise or problem. God honors His word, and He gives freely when we give of ourselves. Pastor Rick Warren once said he tried to outgive God and couldn't, God always returned more.

But the Bible doesn't say we can have everything; it says we can have anything. "Everything" takes no effort. "Anything" requires focus and purpose. I may not have tens of millions, but I have fulfillment. Give freely, stay grounded, and trust the promise more than the problem.

CORNER QUESTIONS

1. Who's really in your corner, and who's just leaning on the ropes with you?

2. How do you protect your peace when the noise gets loud?

3. What mentor's voice do you still hear when things get tough?

Me with coach Derrick James—sharpening the skills that would carry me into the pros.

Winning doesn't feel real until you've bled for it.

A belt is a receipt—the work is the real reward.

Under the lights—proving I belonged there.

PART III
AFTER THE BELL

"When the bell rings for the last time, your fight with purpose begins."

The bell might stop the round, but it never stops the fighter. The damage to my vision ended one chapter, but it opened another. These final rounds are about what happens after the applause fades, where the real fight for faith, family, and meaning begins.

After the bell—the fighter, the coach, and the man, stepping into a new season with the same heart, just a different purpose.

THE PIVOT

"Sometimes life throws in the towel for you, pivot anyway."

What matters is what you do when you turn the corner. Losing my sight didn't just end my career; it ended the version of myself I believed I'd always be. One day, I was training for the next big fight, and the next, I was staring at a ceiling I could barely see, wondering what was left of the man I'd built. Boxing had always been my purpose, my discipline, my identity. When it was gone, I felt like I'd been thrown into the middle of a round with no idea how to defend myself. I'd never felt that kind of confusion hit so fast.

The first few weeks were a blur of frustration. I couldn't sit still. The quiet was too loud. My body still craved the rhythm of training: the sweat, the sound of the bag, the pace of the bell, but my mind had nowhere to put that energy. I had no income, no plan, and no sense of what came next. I was scared, but I didn't have the luxury of staying down. Survival didn't give me time to feel sorry for myself.

Bills don't care about your injuries. So by late 2015, I started hustling. My boy Blake King had been making good money with Herbalife, and I figured I could sell shakes as easily as I sold myself in a fight. I jumped in headfirst. I had boxes of product in the backseat of my car and a trunk full of samples. I'd drive across Dallas, knock on doors, and talk to anyone who would listen. It wasn't glamorous, but it gave me structure again. It gave me something to chase. I needed anything that kept me moving.

On those long drives, I started feeding my mind the same way I used to feed my body. Instead of music, I listened to Les Brown, Jim Rohn, and Earl Nightingale, voices that hit harder than any punch. They talked about purpose, about struggle, about the process of becoming. Their words didn't fix my eye, but they fixed my mindset. For the first time, I realized my fight wasn't over; it had just changed arenas. Hearing their voices made me feel like I wasn't climbing alone.

During that rebuilding phase, God started connecting dots I didn't even know existed. I had been training an MMA fighter named Justin, who had a close friend named Tre Powell. Tre had just gone through a tragedy: his father and stepbrother had been murdered back in Pennsylvania. Justin asked if I'd be willing to spend time with him, to keep him grounded. I said yes without hesitation.

What started as helping a friend became one of the biggest blessings of my life. Tre and I hit it off right away, and over time, he became like family. I was the best man at his wedding and godfather to his daughter. It felt good to matter to someone again.

When Tre eventually moved back to Pennsylvania, he handed off a few of his clients to me before he left. One of them was a woman named Heather. At first, she was just another client. She and her friend Kim started coming to class a few times a week, always laughing, always pushing each other. But over time, I realized Heather was special. She was going through a divorce, had battled cancer multiple times, and yet she never once complained. She'd show up anyway, wrap her hands, tie her gloves, and say, "Let's work." Watching her train was like watching courage personified. Seeing her fight made my problems feel smaller.

When things started falling apart at The GYM, a local boxing-fitness spot where I was coaching at the time, I was scared. I knew boxing, but I didn't know business. I didn't want to fail because I didn't understand the parts outside the ring. That's when I approached Heather about teaming up. I trusted her discipline and her consistency. I needed someone steady when I wasn't sure I could be.

We left The GYM together and moved into a space called The Den. That's where TMACK Elite was really born, not because I had a business plan or investors lined up, but because I had someone who believed in me at a time when I barely believed in myself.

We pulled every bag, glove, and mat out of that dying gym before the lights went out, loaded it into Nate's truck, and hauled it to his warehouse. We didn't know what came next, but we knew it was ours to figure out. It felt like starting over, but at least I wasn't alone this time.

We found a small space: cheap rent, low ceilings, cracked mirrors, but it was ours. The first few months were chaos. I was training people from sunrise to sundown, doing everything from cleaning floors to running classes. Heather helped manage clients, run sessions, and bring some order to the madness. She had a way of calming my impulsive side.

Eventually, though, she realized her calling wasn't running a boxing gym. She loved training and yoga, and that's where her heart was. She signed her half of the business over to me and cheered me on from the sidelines. That's one thing about real friends: they don't hold you back when it's your time to grow. Losing her help stung, but her support never faded.

Even with her support, the grind was brutal. The Den, where I was based, had potential, but the ownership was a mess. My boxing classes were the only thing keeping the doors open. Every month felt like a fight to stay above water. Then the building owner decided to sell, and in walked Greg McCoy.

Greg was a year younger than me but miles ahead when it came to business. He was a professional bodybuilder who had already built and sold successful gyms. Most owners are either too controlling or too disconnected, Greg was neither. He noticed who was showing up early, who was staying late, and who actually cared. When he took over, he let most of the staff go, but he kept me. That told me I was doing something right.

That decision changed everything. Greg saw something in me that I hadn't yet seen in myself. He offered me a corner of his new space, just four heavy bags and enough room to run small group sessions. It might not sound like much, but it was a lifeline. I treated that corner like Madison Square Garden. Every class, every client, every rep: I gave it everything. I knew opportunities like that didn't come twice.

Under Greg's leadership, I started learning how to build a business the right way. He was disciplined, organized, and structured, and he shared what he knew without ego. He gave me a copy of *Hustle Harder, Hustle Smarter* by 50 Cent, and that book hit me in the gut. It reminded me that being successful isn't just about outworking people: it's about outthinking them. I started looking at my gym not just as a place to train but as a brand, a system, a movement. It was the first time I saw myself as more than just a coach.

Greg helped expand my world. He introduced me to new circles of business professionals and entrepreneurs—people who thought differently, who weren't afraid to take risks. Separately, I met B.B., the general manager at the Tower Club in Dallas. After I hosted a successful Fight Night event there, he invited me to lunch. Midway through, he leaned in and said, "Tony, you're not in the boxing business. You're in the membership business."

That sentence stuck with me. I thought about it all the way home. He was right: people weren't coming to me just to learn how to throw a punch. They were coming because of the community, the energy, the way being in that gym made them feel. It shifted my entire mindset. I stopped thinking like a fighter and started thinking like a business owner. It was a shift I didn't know I needed until he said it out loud.

That new perspective made me ambitious. I decided to open a second location out in Farmersville. The rent was cheap, and it felt like the next logical step. I imagined two gyms running at once, teams training under my banner, TMACK Elite growing across Texas. But almost immediately, I ran into problems. The location was too far, the community didn't fit, and staffing was a nightmare. Still, my pride wouldn't let me quit. I kept pouring money and energy into it, hoping it would turn around. I didn't want to admit I'd misread the situation.

Then Greg brought in a speaker for our staff meeting: a woman named Michelle Blakely, an abundance coach and business mentor. Within five minutes of her talking, I felt called out in the best way. She spoke about alignment, about course correction, about letting go of things that no longer serve you. It was like she was reading my life out loud.

Closing something isn't quitting, it's clearing space for what's next.

After her session, I reached out and asked to work with her one-on-one. That decision was a turning point. Michelle became a major influence in how I approached leadership and business. She challenged me to stop operating out of fear and to start trusting my instincts. She reminded me that closing something isn't quitting: it's clearing space for what's next. With her guidance, I made the hard call to shut down the Farmersville gym. It hurt my ego, but it saved my momentum.

And wouldn't you know it: almost immediately, everything else started to grow. It was like God had been waiting for me to make room. New members started joining at the main location, opportunities started popping up, and then one day, I got a call from Amari Cooper.

Amari was looking for a new way to train. He'd heard about the gym and wanted to check it out. From the first session, I could tell he was different: quiet, focused, all business. Once he started coming in regularly, people noticed. Soon after, he brought in Micah Parsons. Then Micah brought Dan Quinn, then the Cowboys' defensive coordinator, and before long, the entire defensive line was training at my gym.

It was wild watching it unfold. I'd gone from hustling Herbalife out of my trunk to coaching elite NFL players in a space that used to be a storage room. But I didn't see it as luck: I saw it as timing. Every "no" I'd heard before had been preparing me for that "yes." Part of me still couldn't believe how far things had come.

Working with those guys opened new doors, but it also humbled me. I realized that success doesn't eliminate the fight: it just changes what you're fighting for. Suddenly, I wasn't battling opponents; I was managing growth, leading a team, and protecting a culture. I had to learn how to delegate, how to slow down, how to think beyond myself. It was a different kind of pressure, but it still made me rise.

Michelle kept me grounded during that growth. She helped me implement systems: staff meetings, accountability tools, client tracking all the stuff I used to think I didn't need. Greg was still mentoring me from a business standpoint, and Nate never stopped checking in, reminding me that no matter how big things got, character mattered more than reputation.

Then came the opportunity that brought everything full circle: Team Combat League. When they called to ask if I'd be interested in coaching the Dallas Enforcers, I didn't even have to think twice. I'd spent years fighting to get back into the ring in some way, and here was my chance. Only this time, I wasn't the one fighting. I was the one leading.

That moment hit different. Standing in the corner again: not as a boxer but as a coach—made every setback worth it. The blindness, the losses, the detours they were all part of the same training camp. I just hadn't realized it yet. It felt like the ring had been waiting for me the whole time.

I didn't lose the fight. I just changed corners.

Looking back now, every person, every failure, every conversation fits together like a puzzle. Heather taught me what real strength looks like. Greg showed me how to build something that lasts. B.B. taught me the difference between hustling and leading. Michelle helped me trust timing. Amari and the Cowboys reminded me that preparation meets opportunity.

Losing my eyesight could have been the end of my story: but it wasn't. It was the start of a new round. The punches just looked different now. I wasn't swinging for wins anymore; I was fighting for purpose. I didn't lose the fight. I just changed corners.

REFLECTIONS

EVERYONE LEARNS DIFFERENTLY

> *Your differences are your design. Once you understand how you learn, you can teach others to rise the same way.*

Before we talk about learning, let's face the truth: everyone is different. Skin color, faith, upbringing, mindset, fighting style, we're all built uniquely. You can judge that or accept it, but accepting it makes you more effective with people. We assume others think like us, but most don't. Knowing that upfront helps whether you're teaching life skills or showing someone how to move in the ring.

Looking back, I can see that a lot of what I once viewed as flaws were actually strengths. The struggles I faced in school and on the streets shaped my drive and deepened my faith. Now I get to give back to young men facing the same battles and remind them: I see you. If I found my way, you can too.

LET IT GO TO GROW

> *Some people aren't meant to go the full distance with you. Releasing them makes room for what's next.*

People come and go in our lives all the time. Sometimes we drift apart slowly without realizing it; other times we have to make the tough decision to remove people from our lives.

That was the position I found myself in a few years back with one of the fighters I was training. He was talented, but his attitude was poisoning the gym culture. He'd show up late, disrespect other fighters, and blame everyone but himself when things went wrong. I kept hoping he'd change, but he never did.

One day, I had to sit him down and tell him he couldn't train with us anymore. It hurt. But holding on would've hurt more. Sometimes releasing people makes room for the ones who are supposed to be there. Within a month of letting him go, two new fighters joined who became some of my best students.

GUILT OF SUCCESS

> *Success changes the circle. Don't apologize for growth that others chose not to chase.*

My family doesn't always understand the pressure I carry or the choices I have to make. I've had to miss moments with them to chase the goals I believe God put on my heart. They're not wrong for wanting more time, I get it. But if I don't honor the mission I'm called to, no one will.

Sometimes my growth surprises them. They still see the easygoing kid I used to be. They didn't see the late nights, sacrifices, or internal battles it took to become who I am now. I sharpened myself. I stayed consistent. I built something from nothing.

Growth can create tension, not because my family is against me, but because they're not used to seeing someone break ceilings. Success brings a strange guilt when people expect you to stay who you were. I don't look down on anyone, but growth can make even the people you love uncomfortable.

WHEN THE FIGHT MOVES INSIDE

> *Before I rebuilt a gym, I had to rebuild my mind.*

After the blindness, the first battle wasn't physical, it was mental. I had to relearn how to train without a ring, a bell, or a clear target. I replaced footwork with audiobooks, replaced sparring with self-discipline, and replaced physical conditioning with mindset conditioning. The fight never really stops, it just moves inside. This was the season where I built the mental habits that became the foundation of my future success. Before I rebuilt a gym, I rebuilt the way I thought.

BLESSINGS SHOW UP AS PEOPLE

> *Every blessing came dressed like a person.*

From Tre's friendship to Heather's steadiness to Greg's mentorship to Michelle Blakely calling me out at exactly the right moment, each person was another link in the chain pulling me forward. None of the breakthroughs in this chapter came from luck; they came from alignment. When I shut one door (Farmersville), the right ones opened.

CORNER QUESTIONS

1. What setback forced you to pivot into your purpose?

2. Have you ever outgrown a dream and felt guilty about it?

3. What part of your old self are you still trying to keep in the fight?

With Amari Cooper in Las Vegas after building our training partnership.

Rebuilding outside the ring—turning a career-ending injury into a new hustle, new habits, and a new version of myself.

The grind phase—doing whatever it took to keep moving.

Coach mode—building people while I rebuilt myself.

THE PLAYBOOK

"The same hunger that built the boxer built the businessman."

Every fighter encounters a wall. Faith isn't about avoiding these obstacles but about finding your breath when facing them. I used to believe books weren't meant for someone like me. I'd open a page, gaze at the words, and feel my mind wandering. Letters seemed to dance, and sentences would slip away. Reading wasn't just dull, it felt uncomfortable. I could endure ten rounds with a broken rib, but give me a book, and I'd give up before the first bell. I hated that feeling, getting beat by something nobody else even struggled with. It wasn't just frustration; it was shame. It made me feel like I was already behind before the fight even started.

Back in school, they called it "not applying myself." What they didn't see was that I was trying. I just couldn't make my brain fit the shape the classroom demanded. I wasn't built for sitting still under fluorescent lights while somebody told me to underline the main idea. My brain didn't work like that. It worked in rhythm, in pictures, in motion. Most days it felt like the classroom kept moving and I was the only one trying to play catch-up. I remember pretending I understood just so I wouldn't look slow.

So I built my identity around what came naturally: energy, humor, hustle, heart. That was my language. I could motivate a room before I could summarize a paragraph. And for a long time, that felt like enough. I didn't think I needed books, because I had boxing. I had grit. It was easier to lean on what I was good at than face what scared me.

But here's the truth nobody tells you: if your mind can't stretch, your future can't either. I didn't understand that yet. I thought success was muscle and willpower. I didn't realize it was also literacy, learning to read not just the words on a page but the patterns in life. And little by little, I could feel those patterns pressing on me, like life was asking questions I didn't have the language for yet. That pressure stayed with me even when I tried to ignore it.

And this is where this chapter takes a turn. Because the same way certain coaches showed up at the right moment in my boxing career, certain voices started showing up in my life through pages, music, sermons, and moments that cracked something open in me. I didn't know it at the time, but God was giving me mentors long before I ever met them. Some were authors. Some were musicians. Some were pastors. And all of them were handing me pieces of the playbook I'd eventually write myself.

For the first time, I didn't feel like I had to figure everything out on my own strength. It felt like someone finally turned on a light in a room I'd been stumbling through for years.

Back in 2003, when Kanye West came through, he messed up the whole picture of what a "winner" had to look like. Calm. Clean-cut. Polo shirts. Soft-spoken. People clowned him for not fitting the mold. But *Through the Wire* cut through all that noise, pain turned into purpose. When *The College Dropout* dropped, I felt understood in a way I hadn't before. I wasn't boxing yet, but something in his story spoke to me. He made it okay to be different and still be great.

That was my first spark: maybe my difference wasn't a weakness, maybe it was design. Maybe my brain wasn't broken; maybe it just learned in another gear. That spark didn't fix anything overnight, but it gave me permission to stop seeing myself as defective. His music hit me at a time when I was still trying to figure out where I fit in the world. Hearing him made me feel seen before I even knew what I was chasing.

The real breakthrough didn't come from school. It came from a book I never planned to finish. Greg McCoy handed me 50 Cent's *Hustle Harder, Hustle Smarter* and said, "You'll see yourself in this. And when you finish it, come tell me what you learned." I laughed, up to that point, I had never finished a book cover to cover. But page by page, that book started talking to me. Discipline. Strategy. Turning fear into focus. No fluff, just power you could use.

I remember opening it with that old fear creeping in, the fear that I'd quit halfway and prove myself right about not being a "reader." Finishing that book felt like stepping through the ropes for the first time all over again. I realized how much I'd been leaving on the table because I'd labeled reading "not for me." By the time I closed that back cover, something had shifted. I wasn't the same person who opened page one.

I hadn't felt that proud of myself in a long time, like I finally won a fight I'd been losing since childhood. I wasn't just a fighter who read a book. I was a man who had just found a new weapon. It reminded me that growth hits different when you stop running from the things that used to beat you.

And this is where everything changed. Reading didn't just open a door; it kicked it off the hinges. It was like discovering a new style of training, mental conditioning instead of physical conditioning. And because I finally had one book I connected with, it made me curious about the next one. And the next. And the next. My mind finally felt like something I could trust, not something I had to fight.

Books became the mentors I didn't know I was missing.

For the first time, learning didn't feel like punishment; it felt like progress. From there, I went hard: thirty to forty books, front to back. Not skimming. Studying. Applying. Testing the ideas in real time. Books became my new sparring partners. They made my mind quicker, my voice cleaner, my thinking sharper. They gave me confidence on a headset and a microphone, commentating fights, doing interviews, showing up on radio and podcasts, and they made me a better coach because I could explain the "why," not just the "what."

50 also forced me to face the guilt I carried about outgrowing where I came from. He talked about Jam Master Jay and Nipsey Hussle, legends who stayed close to lift others and paid for it with their lives. His takeaway? Don't get trapped where you started. Bring your community with you, but don't let loyalty become a leash.

That landed in a place I'd never touched before. That guilt had been in my chest for years, and I didn't even know it had a name. That gave me permission to grow without apology. Hearing that lifted a weight I didn't realize I'd been carrying.

Then Nate introduced me to Pastor Keith Craft, whose book *Your Divine Fingerprint* gave me language for something I had felt but never named: everybody has a one-percent factor, a divine fingerprint, that makes you unstoppable when you live aligned with it. Honor. Attitude. Excellence. Leadership. Generosity. That five-piece combo became a daily practice. It was the first time I could actually see the man I wanted to become, clearly, not just in flashes.

He taught me that faith and business aren't separate corners. Add value first; money follows. That flipped my whole approach to TMACK Elite. Clients stopped being transactions. They became purpose. Reading didn't just give me ideas; it gave me a framework for who I wanted to be while I built. It felt like someone finally handed me a blueprint instead of telling me to figure it out alone.

And those lessons forced me to look at myself differently, not just as someone being shaped by mentors, but as someone learning how to lead others the same way. It was the first time I realized growth isn't real until you can pass it on.

But a framework is only as strong as the person committed to building from it. That's when I started realizing something deeper: mentors will only take you so far if you're not willing to be accountable for what you learn. Growth isn't just about who pours into you, it's about who you become as a result. And accountability hits different when you know exactly where you've fallen short before.

Somewhere along that journey, God showed me another truth: everyone needs three types of people in their life if they want to keep rising. You need someone you pour into, someone who walks beside you, and someone far ahead who challenges your excuses just by existing. And once I saw that clearly, I had to be honest about who I listened to, and who I shouldn't anymore. The wrong voices can slow you down as fast as the right ones can lift you.

I learned the first category, mentees, by accident. Young men would come into my gym looking for direction, discipline, or just a place to belong. At first, I thought I was only teaching them to throw a jab or slip a punch. But mentorship isn't about technique; it's about accountability on both sides. And when somebody looks at you like you're the person who can change their life, it makes you step up in ways you didn't know you had. If they showed up, followed through, and respected the work, I owed them my best. Their effort pulled the best out of me. Their hunger sharpened my leadership. Mentorship is a mirror; it shows you who you really are.

The second category, the peers, kept me honest. In boxing, it was the guys grinding at my same level, pushing through the same drills, the same pain, the same dreams. In business, it became the gym owners and promoters who weren't famous yet but were clawing their way upward. Watching them push through their own struggles reminded me that I wasn't the only one fighting battles nobody else could see. You learn fast that iron sharpens iron, but only if both pieces are willing to feel the friction. Peers remind you that you're not alone, and that you can't slack. Their grind pushed me in ways comfort never could.

And then there's the third category: the people ten steps ahead. The ones whose presence alone forces you to level up. Most people never put themselves in rooms where they're the least accomplished person there. But those are the rooms that changed me the most. I used to walk in quiet, feeling like everyone else spoke a language I hadn't learned yet. Every insecurity I carried showed up in those rooms, but those same rooms grew me faster than comfort ever could. Over time, the discomfort wasn't a warning, it was confirmation I was exactly where I needed to be. Growth doesn't happen in comfort zones. It happens in the rooms that scare you.

I thought the three-tier framework was complete. Mentees, peers, mentors, that covered everyone. But as TMACK Elite grew and I started hiring people, I realized there's a fourth category I'd been missing: the people who work for you. Not beneath you, for you. Their insight matters. Their perspective matters. Their trust matters. Leadership isn't about standing above people; it's about standing responsible for them. When you nourish your people, they flourish. When you ignore them, they shrink. Accountability goes down the ladder just as much as it goes up. Leading people showed me every place I still had work to do, and that was humbling in the best way. It taught me that leadership isn't earned once, it's earned daily.

That shift, understanding mentorship as a circle instead of a ladder, changed the way I ran my business, my relationships, and my purpose. It made me more intentional with the voices I let close and the voices I listen to from a distance. And it made me see clearly: becoming teachable is what turns a student into a leader. That shift in how I saw mentorship changed the way I listened to every voice God put in front of me, which is why the next book hit me the way it did.

Somewhere in that same season, my business coach, Michelle Blakely, put me on to Jen Sincero's *You're a Badass at Making Money*. Her voice was bold, funny, and straight to the point. She took "money mindset" out of the clouds and dropped it right into daily choices. And truthfully, money was an area where I'd always played smaller than I needed to, because wanting more used to feel wrong. Any time I felt lack, time, money, momentum, her message brought me back: You already have enough to begin. It was the first time I realized wanting more didn't make me ungrateful. It made me honest.

She also changed the way I named failure. When I closed my second gym, I wanted to call it quitting. Through her lens, it became a course correction. That gym closing hurt deep. I carried that loss in silence because I didn't want anyone to see me question myself. That phrase took the shame out and put the steering wheel back in my hands. Not failure, feedback. Not the end, an angle change. That's abundance: trusting there's more ahead when you let go of what isn't working. Letting go felt like losing until I finally saw what it made room for.

Marie Forleo once said, "To be responsible, keep promises to others. To be successful, keep promises to yourself." And that line turned the spotlight back on me, on the promises I broke to myself long before I ever broke them to anyone else. That hit like a punch I didn't see coming. Keeping promises to myself means showing up even when nobody's watching. It's what separates discipline from desire.

John Maxwell's *Developing the Leader Within You* added the guardrail: the moment you think you've arrived, growth stops. No matter how far I've come, from Pleasant Grove to a thriving gym, I'm still a student. Leadership isn't knowing everything; it's knowing when to listen and who to learn from. So I keep people around me who are older with wisdom, peers who keep me honest, and younger grinders who see angles I might miss.

Sure, "manifestation" gets tossed around, but for me it isn't wishing, it's training. *The Power of Your Subconscious Mind* by Dr. Joseph Murphy taught me that thoughts carry energy, but without discipline that energy scatters. Belief without work is noise. Work without belief burns out. You need both: faith in the unseen and a plan you can measure. And for me, this was the season where the main fight wasn't outside, it was in my head. Some days the mental rounds felt harder than anything I ever did in the ring.

Over time, I built a small practice that keeps me aligned: I write to my subconscious and to God about why I believe I deserve what I'm building. It sounds simple, but it forces me to be specific, what I want, why I want it, and what I'm willing to do for it. It also quiets the part of my conscious mind that tries to sabotage me with doubt.

You have to train your thoughts like you train muscles, daily, deliberately, with repetition, until your mind stops arguing with your purpose. It became my way of sparring with the parts of myself that used to slow me down.

And here's where everything in this chapter connects back to this book:

- If I never learned how to train my mind, this book wouldn't exist.
- If those authors and mentors never poured into their pages, I'd have nothing to pour into mine.
- If I never finished that first book, I'd still be carrying the old belief that reading wasn't for me, and this entire project would feel impossible.

I used to think reading wasn't for me. Now it's one of my biggest advantages. I don't read to finish books, I read to change from them. I slow down when a line hits. I sit with a paragraph. I'll circle, re-read, and apply one idea before I move on to the next. I keep a short list of "return books" I cycle back to when I feel drift:

I don't read to finish books, I read to change from them.

- 50 Cent for edge and execution
- Keith Craft for alignment and values
- Jen Sincero for abundance and reframing
- Marie Forleo for integrity
- John Maxwell for leadership
- Dr. Joseph Murphy for belief backed by work

Different rounds, different corners, same fight.

And here's what surprised me most: the more I read, the more free I feel. I'm not chasing random opportunities. I pick the ones that match my design. I don't have to say yes to everything. I finally understand who I am, what I'm building, and why.

Kanye taught me that being different is a strategy, not a flaw. 50 taught me to turn fear into focus and to grow without guilt. Pastor Keith Craft taught me to build with values and add value first. Jen Sincero taught me abundance and course correction. Marie Forleo taught me to keep promises to myself. John Maxwell taught me to stay teachable. Murphy taught me to align belief with measurable work.

And now I see the truth clearly: I didn't become someone else. I became who I was designed to be, on purpose, on page, and still in the fight. Standing here now, with the clarity I once prayed for, I didn't just read my way into this. I grew my way into it.

REFLECTIONS

LET THE DOTS CONNECT

> *Books don't give you the whole path, just the next step.*

So many things in my life unfolded in ways I never thought possible, and I credit a lot of that to rolling with the punches. I've always had vision and determination, but I never mapped out every method for getting there. That might sound counter to what business experts advise, but my belief in myself, and my faith that God would guide me, has served me well. You can be so focused on how that you lose sight of where and why.

If I had sat down and plotted every step to start TMACK Elite, I don't think I would have accomplished a fraction of what I have. You don't need to know the route to trust the guidance. Books became the mentors I didn't know I was missing. Mentors don't have to know your name to change your life.

TRUST IN THE PLAN

> *You don't need to know the route to trust the guidance.*

Whenever life felt impossible, I remembered a parable I heard as a kid. In heaven, a man is shown a room full of wrapped gifts, blessings God meant for him but he never opened because he was too afraid to try. From that day on, I promised myself I'd die empty. No gifts left behind.

The path you take won't always match the plan. Mine didn't. I wasn't the most talented or the most prepared, but when boxing found me, it lit something in me. That spark carried me farther than I expected and later opened the door to entrepreneurship.

Starting doesn't require money or connections, just discipline and belief. Some things are beyond your control, but showing up is always your choice. Every relationship, every setback, every detour prepared me. When the road gets hard, remember: don't leave your gifts wrapped.

EMBRACE CHANGE

> *Transformation isn't betrayal. You were never meant to stay who you were yesterday.*

I've heard people blame their environment for who they are, using it as an excuse for failure. Having lived what I lived, I can't buy into that. Plenty of people around Dallas had similar opportunities to mine, even within my own family. Some were given the chance to step into a different school system, a different environment, but timing and circumstances didn't line up for them the way they did for me.

Even writing that takes me back to that day with the pastor, and I can't deny that God's hand has been on my life from the beginning. The same God who put that blessing over me at twelve years old was the same God who closed one door so another could open. Change isn't something that happens to you. It's something you grow into when you stop resisting it.

BREAK THE CYCLE

> *Growth multiplies when you lift others. Unity beats division, especially within your own community.*

I'm a proud Black man who loves where he comes from, but I don't see life in strict Black-and-White terms. We're all made in God's image and deserve the same dignity. Staying open-minded, about people, help, and growth, keeps you from getting boxed in. That mindset helped me learn from those who expanded my vision and pushed me to think bigger than my surroundings.

I've been given opportunities many never get, and I don't take that lightly. In the gym, I've seen talented fighters lose momentum simply because they couldn't afford to compete. When someone shows up daily with heart and discipline, I don't want money to block their path. I can't help everyone, but I help as many as I can, that's how I give back.

THE INTERNAL STRUGGLE

> *Your biggest opponent lives in the mirror. Win that fight, and everything else falls into place.*

I was so used to losing in boxing that it wore on me. After all the work I put in, I felt like I deserved some success, at least a little respect. Being called "the boxer," especially by people who once picked on me, felt good. I got attached to that title and the pride that came with it. Hearing my older cousins, the ones I admired, say they were proud meant even more.

I pushed myself to prove people wrong, but that pressure cut both ways. If someone came to see me fight, I felt like I had to win. Losing meant carrying that weight alone. Nobody ever shamed me, I created the disappointment in my own head. That's the line between leveling up and burning out.

And that's when I learned the truth: your biggest opponent is always the person in the mirror. Win that fight, and everything else starts to line up.

CORNER QUESTIONS

1. Which person or book has shaped you the most without ever meeting you?

2. What belief did you inherit from your environment that you now realize you can outgrow?

3. What's one lesson from someone you admire that you haven't applied yet?

Les Brown and Keith Craft pouring into me.

Books became my new sparring partners—training my mind like my body.

Pastor Keith Craft—a mentor who pushed my faith and my mindset higher.

Hustle Harder, Hustle Smarter—the first book that changed my trajectory.

THE STABLE

"The measure of a man isn't what he builds alone, it's who helped him build it."

These are the deep rounds. The ones where everything hurts, your lungs burn, your legs feel like cement, and the only thing left swinging is whatever you built on the inside. This is the part nobody glamorizes because it's not pretty, not motivating, and not Instagram friendly. This is where the spotlight dies and your character takes over. This is where your real corner gets exposed. Who shows up. Who disappears. Who claps from a distance. Who steps into the ring with you.

People can talk all day about being self-made. I hear it all the time. They puff their chest out like doing everything alone makes them stronger. That's bullshit. Nobody is self-made. Not a single person walking this earth got where they are without help, without influence, without somebody holding them together when life tried to tear them apart. I learned early that standing alone feels tough until you actually have to do it.

Books changed my mindset, sure. They sharpened me, gave me new language, gave me tools. But PEOPLE? People are the reason I'm alive. People are the reason I didn't fold. People are the reason I knew

Nobody is self-made. Not a single person walking this earth got where they are without help.

how to use those tools in the first place. God didn't build me through comfort. He built me through CONNECTION. Through difficult people, loyal people, broken people, wise people, people who disappointed me, people who held me, people who carried me, and people who forced me to change when I would've stayed the same. Every chapter of my life has someone's fingerprints on it.

Because the truth is, relationships are currency. You can lose money and make it back. You can lose followers and gain them again. But relationships? Real ones? They make you or break you. They open doors no degree can. They save you from decisions that could ruin everything. They shape your character in ways you don't even recognize until years later.

In every chapter of my life, the turning point wasn't a punch, or a paycheck, or a promoter. It was always a PERSON. A real human being who shifted something in me. That's why this chapter isn't just a thank-you. It's the blueprint. The foundation. People carried me further than talent ever could.

My family was the first evidence that God was putting the right people around me way before I knew what I needed. Pops could hustle circles around anybody. The man had charm, unpredictability, charisma, and an ability to talk his way out of anything. He had the engine. He had the drive. He had every raw ingredient of success except the belief that he could go further. So I took his grind, but I refused to inherit his fear. I love him. I always will. But he's also a reminder that talent without evolution becomes a trap. Watching him gave me permission to outgrow what didn't serve me. I didn't want to become a man that stopped at "almost."

My mom and I took the scenic route to a relationship. We went from years of barely talking to now hearing from her more than my accountant. She checks in about the gym, asks if I'm eating, tells me she's proud.

None of that erases the past, but it proves relationships can heal in ways you never expect. That's what people don't understand, sometimes the village you need is the same village that hurt you, because healing is part of the building. Forgiveness is a kind of currency too. Her voice hits different now because I know what it cost us to get here.

Teachers were the next miracle. I wasn't the kid anybody thought would grow into a leader. I was funny. Loud. The entertainer. The one people liked having around but didn't take seriously. Then God put Mrs. Bray and Mrs. Townsend in my path. They saw something in me that didn't show up on report cards. Mrs. Bray told me I wasn't broken; I just learned differently. She said it with conviction like she was speaking life over me. Mrs. Townsend threw me into advanced English like she was daring the world to underestimate me again.

Then the craziest thing happened years later, she started messaging me for BUSINESS advice. Imagine that. The kid nobody took seriously in class, helping a teacher make moves. And Mrs. Bray still cheers me on Facebook like she's been waiting on this version of me since day one. Those women didn't just teach me, they invested in me. They placed belief in my account long before I had anything to withdraw. Their belief hit me harder as an adult than it ever did as a kid.

Then there's Pleasant Grove. Hard to explain unless you lived it. The hood didn't care whether you were smart or talented or funny. It cared whether you could read a room fast enough to stay alive. That place built instincts in me no coach could ever teach. The cracked concrete, the corner stores, the porch lights that stayed on all night, the danger that never clocked out, it shaped my awareness, my hunger, my urgency. And the people in it? They were complicated and loyal and flawed and protective all at once. I didn't realize those instincts would save me in rooms far beyond the neighborhood.

Pooh was like an unofficial security guard assigned to me by God Himself. He protected me in ways I didn't even realize were protection until I looked back years later. Life hit him with losses that would crush most people, his mom, dad, sister, and grandma, all gone before he turned forty. He didn't get the escape route I did. No Aunt San. No new school system. No do-over. And still, he supports me in the only way he knows how, through small gestures, quiet loyalty, and consistency that never changed. People look down on "small" support, but sometimes that's all someone has left to give. And it still counts. Some love whispers and still saves you.

One of my cousins stepped in during a situation that could've ended both of us. That moment taught me that some relationships are lifelines. Even the dangerous ones. Even the imperfect ones. People saved me from consequences I didn't even see coming. Looking back, I used up more grace than I earned.

Chicago was a different kind of classroom. The hustle gene runs deep in my family there. Marc was the closest thing I had to a mirror, same jokes, same energy, same way of moving through rooms. Aunt Jackie built a multimillion-dollar daycare with nothing but grit and vision. She is the definition of taking limited resources and flipping them into possibility. She always told me success meant you kept going when everybody else sat down. That line sits in my chest like cement every time guilt tries to talk me into shrinking my progress just to make others comfortable. She made me believe I could build something bigger than my beginnings.

Some family still doesn't take me seriously. That used to hurt bad. Especially knowing most of the loudest opinions came from people who never lifted a finger to help me. But time humbles people. And one day, when a cousin I'd always looked up to said, "I didn't know you had this kind of discipline," it felt like a weight finally dropped off my shoulders. Sometimes respect shows up late, but it still lands.

The gym brought brothers into my life who shaped me as much as any family member. Robert Brant beating me by 13 points crushed me at the time, but it also forced me into a new level of hunger. We trained together for years, going to war in ways most people will never understand. Blood, sweat, exhaustion, pushing each other until our bodies gave out. Now he's a firefighter and still teasing me about that damn 13 points. That's what brotherhood looks like, competition, respect, and jokes that never get old. He pushed me past limits I didn't even know I had.

Cam F. Awesome came in loud, bold, talking big, acting big, an atheist, hilarious, and charismatic. Watching me and Nate go through our spiritual walks cracked something open in him. Now he motivates half the country with that same voice. We still hype each other up like two kids trying to change the world with nothing but belief. He's family too. He reminded me that influence doesn't require perfection.

And then there was Rashad, whose relationship with me was both messy and necessary. When we met, he was ego walking on two legs, big personality, bigger chip on his shoulder. He was training to become an MMA fighter and came to me and Nate to tighten up his boxing. I was still fighting at the time, so we became sparring partners. I was hesitant at first, because MMA guys sometimes carry a certain energy, like they already know they can knock out the room.

But Rashad backed his confidence up. The first time he got called up for a main event, he ended up winning a $50,000 purse. Along the way, we started hanging out and became real friends. After I retired, I even coached him for a bit. And the closer we got, the more we butted heads, two competitive dudes with no off switch.

Here's what makes it wild: Rashad is also the reason I met Ashley. One night, he pulled me out with him, and that was the first time I ever crossed paths with the woman who would become my wife. I've had to remind myself of that more than once, because life doesn't always send a blessing wrapped in easy packaging.

After Ashley and I got married, Rashad crossed a line. He started saying disrespectful stuff about my wife, and instead of handling it with patience, I reacted on pride and instinct. I told him he wasn't welcome around me, my wife, or my gym. Hurt hits different when it comes from someone you once trusted.

Two years passed. Nate told me Rashad had changed. I didn't want to believe it, most people don't. But he did. Rashad apologized face-to-face to my wife. She forgave him. And if she could forgive him, I didn't have a choice. Sometimes grace reopens doors pride keeps closed.

He became one of the hardest-working, most dependable men in my life. He rebuilt my entire ring one night just to surprise me. That's love. That's loyalty. That's someone God sent back into my life on purpose. Brotherhood is messy, inconvenient, emotional, but it's real. I learned that restoration can be stronger than the original bond.

And then comes Ashley. My wife. My center. My grounding. My peace. My home. She is the reason I didn't spiral when life knocked the wind out of me. She's not in the gym running mitts or teaching classes, but she's behind every victory I've had since we met. She keeps me focused when the noise gets loud. She keeps me steady when stress tries to break me. She is the definition of a partner, quiet strength, steady presence, consistent love. I decided early that I was loyal to her, and that loyalty shaped my reputation, and that reputation shaped my business, and that business shaped our life. Coming home to her is my favorite part of the day. She is my undefeated record. Support doesn't have to be loud to be real.

When I look at everything, every wound, every lesson, every person, I don't see struggle anymore. I see structure. A framework made of people. A stable full of relationships that carried me, corrected me, challenged me, and changed me. Relationships are the real currency. They build fortunes no bank can touch. They create opportunities degrees can't buy. They shape character no motivational talk can imitate. And every blessing I've received in life came attached to a person God placed in my path at the exact right moment. My story isn't built on wins, it's built on people.

My story isn't built on wins, it's built on people.

If one of my young fighters starts blaming their past or their parents or their neighborhood, I shut it down quick. You don't get to hide behind pain. You fight through it. I could've stayed in Pleasant Grove. I could've quit after my eye injury. I could've folded so many times it's embarrassing to think about. But people pulled me out. People called me higher. People wouldn't let me settle. And because they held me up, I get to hold other people up now. The village that raised me is the village I now protect.

It takes a village to build a fighter. It takes a lifetime to build a man. And I'm still learning, still growing, still becoming. Growth didn't stop when success showed up, it got louder.

The older I get, the more I understand that everything I've built came through people, through the ones God placed in my life to guide me, sharpen me, pull me forward, and sometimes put me back together. I didn't climb out alone. I didn't rise alone. I didn't succeed alone. And I damn sure won't go into the next chapter alone. Nothing I have stands without the hands that lifted me.

When I think about what's next, my mind goes straight to relationships. They've been the turning point in every chapter of my life. If God built me through people, then the next thing I build has to honor that.

REFLECTIONS

PRACTICE WHAT YOU PREACH

> *Integrity means alignment. Say it, live it, and let people see it in your work.*

I've been blessed with mentors and role models who guided me along the way. I wouldn't be where I am without the support of my family, coaches, managers, trainers, and friends. Because I've been given so much, I make it a priority to give back, through tithing and by investing time into young men who need direction.

I've always had a way of connecting with people, especially young men who see their own story in mine. Growing up the way I did, they know I understand their challenges. I was fortunate to have an aunt who placed me in a better environment and opened doors I couldn't open on my own. With faith, hard work, and consistency, anyone can rise above their circumstances. That's the example I try to set.

INCLUDE THE OUTSIDER

> *Invite others in, the ones left out might bring the breakthrough you need.*

Maybe it's because of what I've lived through, but I believe everyone deserves a real chance if they're willing to show up and work. I don't care where you come from or what mistakes you've made, everyone has a purpose. In my gym, we treat people like family. We don't judge their past. My faith teaches me to accept people and help them grow. If Jesus could sit with tax collectors and outcasts, I can give someone a fresh start.

One of our biggest success stories is Rock, who came to train after eighteen years in prison. He took accountability, rebuilt his life, and now he has a family, a gym, a charity, and a book. That doesn't erase his past, it shows what's possible when someone truly wants to change. Inclusion is about giving people a path forward.

THE POWER OF WOMEN

> *Strong men are built by strong women. Respect, partnership, and gratitude elevate everyone.*

I have to start with my Aunt San, she was more than an aunt; she was like a mother to me. She opened her home in Plano and literally saved my life. If she hadn't given me a place to stay, I don't know if I would have survived Pleasant Grove the way I did, and I know I wouldn't have the career I have today. Aunt Shay taught me how to learn when the world wanted me to believe I was the problem; her unorthodox methods gave me confidence I still rely on.

Then there's Aunt Jackie, who ran a daycare and kept the family close through reunions. She built a business from the same rough section of Chicago many of us came from and kept hustling even after others around her found success. These women shaped me: stability, lessons, and quiet strength. I'm deeply grateful for all they did and continue to do.

THE FOUR PILLARS OF PEOPLE

> *Surround yourself with mentors, peers, learners, and dreamers, each one holds up a corner of your purpose.*

I heard a message from Pastor Rick Warren that changed the way I think about people: we all need four kinds of people to thrive, mentors, models, partners, and friends. One person can fit multiple pillars, but each role provides different support. I couldn't have done what I did without those pillars in my life, and I'm grateful for every one of them.

Think big and look for inspiration in unexpected places. These pillars aren't just labels, they're the framework that helped me grow. Mentors teach, models show the way, partners share the grind, and friends keep you grounded. Value them.

IT TAKES A VILLAGE

> *No legacy stands alone. Community is the true measure of any champion.*

Outside of my Pops, so many people played crucial roles while I was growing up and still do. Family and teachers came together to support my ambitions and never backed down, even when the odds were against me. Not everyone has that luxury, but too many who do fail to see it. At a young age, it's easy to view elders as only authority figures instead of the helpers they can be. I'm grateful for every positive influence I had.

Because of that village, I feel accomplished and proud. Boxing has taken me around the world, Beijing, Manchester, Mexico, and it all started with moments like winning Class President. I now run a top-ranked gym in the DFW area, work with champions and kids, and try to pass forward the same village that lifted me.

CORNER QUESTIONS

1. Who are the "four corners" in your own life, the people who hold you up when you can't stand alone?

2. Which relationship taught you the hardest lesson about forgiveness or faith?

3. How do you honor the people who invested in you, even when they can't see the outcome?

4. What does "community" look like for you right now, and how can you strengthen it?

5. How can you become someone else's corner today?

Ashley and me—my peace, my partner, my home base.

Family support—the kind of love that holds you together.

Grandma, my aunts, Ashley, and me—the women who kept me grounded.

Legacy and lineage—the corner I come from.

Cam—Not just training partners, but brothers who kept each other grounded between the rounds of life.

Rashad—proof that growth can come back around when pride gets out of the way.

Heather—steadiness in the early grind, and the kind of support that helps a vision breathe.

Nate—the mentor who sharpened my thinking when I was still learning the business rounds.

WATCHING THE FILM

"Clarity doesn't come in the fight. It comes after."

When the lights fade, the crowd goes home, and the sweat dries, there's one thing left that separates the amateurs from the champions: watching film. Every fighter says they'll do it. Most don't. They don't want to see the truth. The film doesn't care about your excuses, your hype, or your version of the story. The film shows what really happened. The tape exposes you, but it also teaches you if you can get past the embarrassment long enough to study it. I hated how honest that screen could be. Nothing humbles you faster than seeing yourself without the excuses.

I've been watching the tapes of my life lately. Not the highlight reels, but the raw footage. The parts I used to fast-forward. The parts I didn't want to look at. The moments I blamed on other people, or timing, or bad luck, or whatever excuse made me feel better at the time. Watching it back now, with distance, age, and purpose, everything looks different. Slowing down the footage changes the whole meaning. It's wild how truth hits different when you finally stop running from it.

When I rewind the early rounds of my life, I can see it clearly now: God wasn't building a boxer. He was building a teacher. Boxing was just the language He used to reach me.

I used to think my childhood disadvantages made me less than. I wasn't the smartest kid. Reading was a struggle. I stuttered. I couldn't sit still. Pops wasn't into medication, so I had to make do with what I had. But watching the tapes, I see something I couldn't see then. All those "disadvantages" weren't weaknesses, they were muscles. They made me pay attention. They made me curious. They made me watch people closely. They made me listen with intention. They made me ask "why" until I understood. Those traits didn't make me a better student; they made me a better coach. Back then I thought I was surviving; turns out I was being shaped.

When I watch my old sparring footage, I laugh at how many questions I used to ask Nate and my coaches. Why this angle? Why this footwork? Why this combination? Why this drill? I must've driven him crazy. But he never shut me down. He let me ask. He taught me how to connect the dots. That curiosity became part of my DNA. It's why I can't just train somebody, I have to teach them. I have to explain the "why" behind the "what." That started back in those early rounds, long before I knew I was being molded. I learned more between punches than I ever did throwing them.

The tapes also show how fast the lights can mess with you. Under the big arena lights, when ten thousand people scream your name, your ego starts throwing punches too. You think you're built different. You think the rules don't apply to you. You think you're invincible. But the camera doesn't lie: I was still the same Tony who showed up to spar at dawn. And staying grounded saved me from becoming the man I swore I'd never be. Deep down I knew the lights didn't mean I'd already arrived.

Losing my vision feels different in the replay. Back then, I told everybody I was fine, but I wasn't. I was scared in a way I didn't have words for yet. Fighters don't admit fear, we tape over it and keep swinging. But that season? I was waking up every day pretending I wasn't losing the one thing my whole identity was built on. It didn't happen in one moment or one fight, it happened over years. Every round, every jab I slipped late, every shot I took added up until the doctor finally told me the truth: the damage had been building all along.

At the time, it felt like the end. But watching it back now, I can see it was the beginning. I see fear on my face, but I also see clarity. I see God closing a door before the room collapsed on me. If I had kept fighting blind, I would've taken damage that no surgery could fix. The injury didn't ruin my life, it rerouted it. And if I had stayed in the ring, there's a real chance I never would have found my real fight: helping other people rise. I didn't understand it then, but losing the ring gave me my real vision.

When I watch the tapes of my losses now, I see them differently. Back then, every stumble felt like confirmation that something was wrong with me, that I wasn't strong enough, smart enough, disciplined enough. Every time I lost a fight, I told myself I let everyone down. My trainers. My family. My friends. The people who drove miles to watch me. Nobody ever said I disappointed them, that voice was mine. I carried that guilt like it was part of the uniform.

Looking at that footage today, I don't see disappointment. I see a kid who wanted to give people a win so badly that he carried a weight that never belonged to him. I see a fighter who didn't understand yet that losing wasn't failure; losing was feedback. Loss wasn't proof I wasn't meant for something, loss was God's way of strengthening the parts of me talent could never touch.

Failure looks different in the replay. It's slower. Truer. Less brutal than it felt in real time. Every setback sharpened something in me, my patience, my discipline, my faith. Losing didn't break me. It built me. Every "no" that crushed me at the time eventually became a doorway to a version of myself I wasn't ready for yet. It just took time for me to see that door instead of the wall.

Champions aren't the ones who never fall. They're the ones who refuse to stay down. That's what these tapes taught me: every round I thought was the end was actually the beginning of who I was becoming. Every loss was a setup for a different version of me I couldn't see yet.

Champions aren't the ones who never fall. They're the ones who refuse to stay down.

And when I look at the tapes from my transition into business, it's like watching a whole different fighter learn a whole different sport. My circle got smaller, but my accountability got sharper. I surrounded myself with people who didn't care about my resume, they cared about my responsibility. People who weren't impressed by what I had done, but invested in who I was becoming. That's leadership. And that's love, even when it doesn't feel like love in the moment. Those were the days I learned the difference between being coached and being carried.

The tapes also show how God uses people in ways you don't expect.

Rashad, the fighter who tested my patience more than anybody, is also the one who introduced me to Ashley. Life is wild like that. I wasn't even planning to meet my wife when I did. But watching that part back? I can see how everything lined up perfectly. Timing, people, placement. Nothing accidental.

Ashley came into my life exactly when I needed a different kind of strength. It still blows my mind how the person I met last became the person I needed first. She became the quiet structure under every loud moment of my career. She's the reason I didn't spiral, the reason I didn't lose myself after I lost the one thing I thought defined me. She doesn't need to be in the ring with me, she anchors me outside of it. Watching those tapes reminds me that real partnership doesn't cheer the loudest; it lifts the heaviest. Her presence hit harder than any belt I ever won.

I've also watched footage of redemption. One of the fighters I trained, Rock, came home after eighteen years in prison. He didn't want pity. He wanted purpose. Watching him rebuild his life one rep, one round, one choice at a time, it taught me more about discipline than any training camp I ever survived. Seeing him show up every day reminded me not to take my second chances for granted. Now he's running his own gym, wrote a book, built a family, created change. When I watch his tapes, I see the power of second chances, real ones. And it reminds me why my doors will always stay open to anyone with heart. Some people just need one clean shot at becoming who they really are.

People think boxing is violence. They don't see the healing. They don't see how a gym becomes a rehab center for emotions nobody ever learned how to name. They don't see a room full of broken people learning to breathe again. Watching the tapes, I can see how many men walked in lost and walked out different, stronger, wiser, freer. And I see now that God didn't give me the gym to build fighters. He gave me the gym to rebuild people.

There's footage from a sparring session early in my career that taught me a lot about respect and assumptions. My coach Paul Vazquez had me work with a seasoned professional boxer, tough, experienced, and technical. I remember trying to take it easy at first, but once she caught me clean, it became real work. That round taught me about respect, control, and how fast the ring exposes what you think you know.

Years later, I learned more about her journey and who she is. It deepened my respect. But the lesson on that tape doesn't change: the ring tells the truth, every time. Labels don't matter here. Your work does. Everyone deserves a place where they can train, grow, and be coached without having to defend who they are before they even throw a punch.

And there are plenty of "coaching tapes" of myself. Days where I didn't want to lead, didn't want to show up, didn't want to problem-solve. Days where staying in bed would've been easier. Watching that back is humbling, because it shows me the truth: it's not talent that separates dreamers from doers. It's discipline. It's accountability. It's showing up when you don't feel like being seen. Some days the only thing I had going for me was that I walked through the door.

Watching the tapes also shows where I changed. Where I learned that being the loudest guy in the room doesn't make you the leader, it makes you insecure. Leadership is listening. Leadership is asking questions. Leadership is learning from people who already walked the path. Leadership is admitting you don't know everything. Watching the tapes makes that obvious.

When I doubt myself, I go back to the footage. I see how many rounds I survived that I shouldn't have. I see how many punches I took that could've put me out. I see how many setbacks turned into setups. And I coach myself the same way I coach my fighters: stop complaining, get up, and get back to work. You don't lose focus because you're tired. You lose focus because you forgot why you started.

If you want the TMACK blueprint, watching the tapes makes it clear:

- Show up.
- Work the problem.
- Play long.
- Stay humble.
- Choose rooms that stretch you.
- Protect your focus.
- Give back.

Watching the tapes proves every one of those principles true. Seeing it all laid out like that reminds me I didn't learn any of this quick.

My faith looks different in the replay too. I see moments where God carried me when I didn't even realize He was in the room. I see blessings I walked right past. I see opportunities I almost ruined. I see doors He shut so I wouldn't walk into disaster. And I see rooms full of unopened gifts I didn't have the maturity to accept at the time. That parable about heaven's warehouse hits different when you realize how many blessings you've walked around because you didn't think you were ready. It makes you wonder how many more were sitting right in front of you.

I used to think I didn't make millions as a fighter because I wasn't good enough. Watching the tapes, I can see I wasn't disciplined enough to handle that kind of money back then. God wasn't withholding, He was protecting. The man I am today, the coach, the mentor, the leader, I wouldn't trade that for ten championship belts. I couldn't have understood that truth back then, not with the mindset I had.

When I watch the full footage of my life, not just the knockouts, but the moments in between, I see the truth: I didn't end up where I planned, but I ended up exactly where I was meant to be. And that's what I try to remind every person who walks into my gym. No matter what round they're in, no matter how tired they are, no matter how many setbacks they're carrying, they still have something left in them. Most people forget that strength doesn't show up until you run out of options.

Don't drop your hands. Don't lose your guard. Don't stop moving. And when the final bell rings, whenever it rings, make sure the tape shows one thing: You gave everything you had. You left nothing on the table.

You die empty. That's the only finish line that ever mattered to me.

You die empty. That's the only finish line that ever mattered to me.

REFLECTIONS

THE POWER OF GIVING AND FORGIVING

> *Giving heals others; forgiving heals you. Both release the weight that holds you back.*

I've always believed that keeping God first brings blessings. One way that shows up for me is in giving. John David Mann's The Go-Giver talks about this, but it's bigger than getting something back, it's the feeling you get from giving. Generosity makes you happy. The more you give, the happier you are.

Giving isn't always easy. I once worried about tithing during a slow month, but I kept my promise and the next month was one of our best. Giving isn't only money, it's time and talent. When I was starting, I gave coaching and mentorship because I had nothing else to give. Now I can give more, and it brings me joy. Forgiveness works the same way: it releases weight and lets you move forward.

KEEPING OPTIONS OPEN

> *Stay flexible with your plan, but firm in your purpose. The open mind wins the long game.*

Things won't always go your way. I've learned that firsthand. As an athlete, your career can end in a blink. That's why so many people preach multiple income streams. I don't mean seven unrelated businesses, that's a distraction. But if you build related streams off your main thing, you create resilience. For me, fighting doesn't have to be the only thing: I can train fighters, teach boxing fitness, promote shows, and build a brand.

Don't put all your eggs in one basket, but also don't chase every shiny thing. Focus on what you're passionate about and diversify around that. Keep options open but stay true to your purpose.

BLOCK THE DISTRACTIONS

> *Focus is a fight of its own. Protect your peace so your purpose can breathe.*

Being a pro athlete brings people out of the woodwork. When you work at Walmart, nobody shows up to hang out, but when you're on a main event card, suddenly everyone wants something. That can be dangerous. My mentor warned me, family, friends, and women can be the most dangerous distractions to a boxer's career. On the night of a fight, those people need to be kept at a distance.

One second of distraction can cost you a block or a step and change everything. Focus is essential, sometimes the difference between walking out and being carried out of the ring. Protect your peace so your purpose can breathe.

NOT ALL IQ IS CREATED EQUAL

> *Smart isn't just books, it's heart, hustle, and awareness. Wisdom beats intellect every time.*

My Pops helped me develop social IQ. He could talk to anyone and make them feel like a friend. I watched and learned, and even though I struggled with reading, stuttered sometimes, and might have had undiagnosed ADD or ADHD, I adapted. I leaned into listening and connecting. That social instinct helped me fit in and build relationships that mattered.

I wasn't going to make it on brains alone, so I used what I had. Thinking critically and listening let me bridge gaps and open doors. Intelligence isn't just books, it's heart, hustle, and the ability to read people. Wisdom beats raw intellect most days.

GROWTH IS A RESPONSIBILITY

> *Elevation isn't escape—it's accountability to what you've learned.*

Becoming better isn't about leaving people behind, it's about raising the standard for what's possible. Growth doesn't disconnect you from your past; it gives you the strength to navigate it with more clarity and compassion. You can honor where you come from without living there. Real leadership means using what you've learned to inspire others, not to judge them. Every season of elevation asks the same question: "What will you do with the wisdom you've earned?" Looking back didn't break me, it built me. I didn't need a new fight. I needed a new perspective.

CORNER QUESTIONS

1. What part of your story looks different when you watch it with honesty instead of judgment?

2. What lesson were you living through long before you understood why?

3. When you look back at your setbacks, what pattern or purpose do you see forming?

In my element at TMACK Training—the same ring that became my classroom.

Me and Pops in the gym, the man who stayed in my corner long after the final bell.

Back to the ropes—reviewing, refining, and staying sharp.

Entrepreneur, mentor, and man of faith—still fighting, just in a different arena.

APPENDIX

BOOKS THAT BUILT ME

These books and voices shaped my mindset, sharpened my discipline, deepened my faith, and helped me grow into the man, coach, and leader I am today. They became mentors long before I ever met the people who wrote or spoke the words.

FAITH AND FOUNDATION

- The Bible
- The Book of Proverbs (Bible)
- *Your Divine Fingerprint*, Keith Craft
- *Chase the Lion*, Mark Batterson

MINDSET AND PERSONAL GROWTH

- *Hustle Harder, Hustle Smarter*, 50 Cent
- *The Power of Your Subconscious Mind*, Dr. Joseph Murphy

AUTHORS AND MENTORS

- John Maxwell
- Jen Sincero
- Marie Forleo

INFLUENTIAL VOICES

- Kanye West
- Les Brown
- Jim Rohn
- Earl Nightingale

EPILOGUE

I pulled the first book because it wasn't ready, and neither was I. I wrote that version like a fighter still swinging at ghosts, still defending old wounds, still trying to prove something. I didn't like the way it felt when I read it back, so I took it off the shelf and went back to work.

The first version was defensive, trying to justify every choice, explain every wound, prove I wasn't the kid people underestimated. This version is different. It's not about proving anything. It's about sharing what I learned so someone else doesn't have to fight as long as I did to figure it out.

This time around, I wrote from a different place. Not pain, perspective. Not ego, experience. Not anger, understanding. When you grow, the story grows with you. And I wanted this version to come from the man I am now, not the kid still trying to outrun his past.

It took two years, a lot of hard conversations with myself, and the kind of patience I didn't know I had. But I'm glad I waited. This version is the truth, not just the facts.

I didn't rewrite this book to fix the past. I rewrote it to honor it. To tell the truth the right way. To give thanks to the people who showed up in the hardest moments and helped me become somebody worth listening to. That's really all this is, my way of saying, "Here's what the fight taught me. Here's what I learned the long way." If somebody wants their version, they can write their own. This one is mine.

Boxing gave me discipline. Life gave me lessons. Writing gave me clarity.

And now that this story is finally out in the world the way it was meant to be, I'm ready for what's next. Whatever that looks like, I know it will involve people, purpose, and the same hunger that got me here. This book is about how I was built—the people, the relationships, the corners that turned potential into purpose.

I'm not done growing. I'm not done learning. I'm not done fighting for the man God is shaping me into. But for now, this chapter closes with peace.

Thank you for reading my story. Thank you for giving it space. And thank you for stepping into the ring with me one more time. The bell just rang. On to the next round.

ABOUT THE AUTHOR

Tony Mack is a USA Certified Boxing Trainer, professional boxing coach, and founder of TMACK Elite Training, TMACK Elite Promotions, and "The Corner: Where Wisdom Meets Work," a mentorship platform where he shares lessons on leadership, discipline, and personal growth.

Known for blending high-level fight strategy with deep mindset, leadership, and character development, Tony has spent more than twenty years shaping athletes into champions, inside and outside the ring.

A former Texas Super Middleweight Champion with a professional record of 13–1–1, Tony competed for the USA National Boxing Team, the World Series of Boxing, and won six Dallas Golden Gloves titles, along with a National Championship.

Today, Tony applies his experience at the highest levels of combat sports, coaching World Title contenders, UFC fighters, and NFL athletes, and serving as Head Coach of the Team Combat League's Dallas Enforcers, where he earned a nomination for Coach of the Year. Beyond boxing, Tony is also a certified personal trainer, a marathon runner, and a physique bodybuilding competitor.

Tony's influence extends far beyond athletics. As a mentor, speaker, and leader, he specializes in teaching wisdom, personal discipline, and mental resilience. His mission is to help people transform setbacks into setups for success, a message captured in his debut book, *Defeat to Destiny: From Setbacks to Success.*

Tony lives in Dallas with his wife, Ashley, where he continues to coach, mentor, and build community through TMACK Elite.

His work has been featured on ESPN/SportsCenter, Sunday Night Football, Inside the NFL, Sports Illustrated, Fox News, NBC News, CBS News, Dallas Morning News, and The Ticket Radio Show.

ACKNOWLEDGMENTS

Writing a book is no easy task. I am beyond grateful to have lived through all the experiences you just read about, but I also realize that along the way, I may not have been able to mention every single person in my life who has made a positive impact. Had I tried, this would be more of an encyclopedia and less of a heartfelt way for me to give back and inspire others to do better, push harder in their own lives.

FAMILY

I would be remiss not to acknowledge my little brother, Kameron Mack. My father's son, Kameron, is my brother and an important part of my family and my journey. Even if I don't talk about him much in these pages, he's a part of my life and deserves to be recognized here.

To my Pops: You gave me discipline, work ethic, and a standard I'm still trying to live up to. You showed me how to fight for what I wanted and how to protect what I built. Everything I am started with you.

I also want to thank Teresa, who has been a steady presence in my life since I was six years old. I'm grateful for the ways you supported me and showed up for me over the years. Your consistency mattered more than you know.

MY WIFE

To my wife, Ashley: You are my peace, my grounding, my home. You've supported me through every transition, every late night, every dream that kept me awake. You don't need the spotlight to be the reason it all works. Thank you for being my corner when I didn't know I needed one.

MENTORS AND FRIENDS

Before I thank anyone else, I have to acknowledge Nate. You've been my manager, my mentor, my business partner, and my friend for over a decade. You saw something in me when I was still trying to see it in myself. You taught me how to think like a businessman while staying true to my values. You've been in my corner through every major decision, every setback, and every victory. I wouldn't be who I am without you. Thank you.

I would also be remiss not to acknowledge my good friend, Brian Burton. If not for Brian, I might not have made this book a reality. He called me one day and very pointedly said, "It's time for the next phase of your life, writing a book. You've done so much with your life in such a short period of time; it's time to inspire others." Going back to my Collin County Community College days, when Brian was the assistant basketball coach, he always looked out for me. He was a young Black man who was running things at the college, and I looked up to him. He treated me like family: every time the basketball players got new uniforms, he gave me new ones. Every time the basketball players got new shoes, he gave me new shoes. His words of motivation were the ultimate inspiration.

Then there's my good friend Shi. Whenever I am going through issues outside of business or boxing, Shi is the guy I turn to. Whether I'm having a problem with my wife, family, or internally, Shi is the guy who will listen without judgment. He'll be the first one to tell me I'm in the wrong when I need to hear it, but he won't scold me or make me feel bad. This is super important to me and is greatly appreciated, because I am used to leaning on Nate for so many things, and having an impartial voice takes the stress off. Nate is more like a spiritual father, and his style of love can come with scolding and a kick in the ass. And while that's good most of the time and has helped me tremendously over the years, it's nice to have other outlets.

I also want to thank Ms. Gail, the mother of my good friend JJ, for the support and kindness she showed me during an important season of my life. I appreciate you.

BOXING FAMILY

I also want to thank Derrick James for the years you invested in me as a trainer. You adapted your teaching style, met me where I was, and pushed me to become a better fighter than I thought I could be. I'm grateful for everything you taught me.

I mentioned my friend Tobius Sims briefly when talking about our sparring session that led to me discovering the detached retina. Tobius likes to tell people that he is the one who detached my retina, which isn't true. He wouldn't want the responsibility for that, and, in reality, he was just the one who brought the underlying issue to the surface. We started as amateur fighters together and remain the best of friends to this day. He now owns a business under the umbrella of Nate's company, and I could not be happier for him. Without boxing putting all the pieces in place, none of this might be possible today.

I need to mention again how amazing Cam is. Yes, his last name is legally 'Awesome.' It's tough to say much more about someone who legally changed his last name to "Awesome," but if anyone I know could fill those shoes, it's Cam. He's a twelve-time national champion and could have achieved so much more in his career if he weren't such a rebel. He was the best amateur heavyweight fighter, and he never trained or worked out. He just stepped into the ring and had fun beating the hell out of people. I still envy that to this day because I would overthink before fighting a tough opponent and forget to enjoy it. Cam had so much fun that he was disqualified from the USA Boxing Olympic team for refusing to follow the strict rules that took the fun out of it. Now, he travels the world as a motivational speaker and continues to be a big source of inspiration in my life, even as I mentor him on his journey. Oh, and he wrote the foreword for this book, in case you forgot!

FAITH

I mention Pastor Keith Craft several times throughout this book, but he deserves a special acknowledgment for turning me onto the second-best faith-based book I have ever read after the Bible. The Power of the *Book of Proverbs* has had such a significant impact on my life, especially when I am struggling. It's thirty-one chapters in total, and each chapter correlates to a day of the month with Biblical wisdom for the personal or business struggles we may be going through. Whenever things seem too difficult to handle, all I need to do is open up to the chapter coinciding with the day of the month we are on, and somehow the answer seems to be perfectly aligned with what I need to hear. We can never have too many tools at our disposal for dealing with challenges and self-doubt.

THE TEAM

Last, but certainly not least, are the people who help me do what I do day in and day out. My staff, my clients, my sponsors, and the fighters I train. I am eternally blessed to have you all in my life, and I am grateful for the faith and trust you place in me to always do what is right for the business and your careers.

DISCUSSION GUIDE

DEFEAT TO DESTINY:
FROM SETBACKS TO SUCCESS
BY TONY MACK II

This guide is designed for book clubs, team meetings, mentorship groups, athletic programs, and individual reflection. Use these questions to spark deeper conversation about the themes in Tony's story and how they apply to your own journey.

Part I: Before The Bell

ROUND 1: DON'T LET YOUR ENVIRONMENT DEFINE YOU

1. Tony writes that his environment could have defined him, but it didn't. What aspects of your own environment have you had to actively resist or reframe?
2. Pops taught Tony the power of a handshake and looking someone in the eye. What small lessons from your upbringing have had an outsized impact on your life?
3. Tony's aunts stepped in to provide stability when his mother couldn't. Who are the unexpected people who showed up for you?
4. How do you balance honoring where you came from while striving for something different?

ROUND 2: THE MAKING OF A FIGHTER

1. Tony was labeled as having a learning disability, but he later realized he just learned differently. How do labels limit our potential?
2. The Bellwether program was designed to help struggling students but ended up isolating them. Have you experienced a system that was meant to help but actually held you back?
3. Tony lost several friends to violence before he was even in high school. How has loss shaped your perspective on life?
4. Tony describes Aunt Shay's tough-love method of drilling him on the Constitution until he could pass. Where's the line between firm discipline and going too far?

ROUND 3: BETWEEN TROUBLE AND A TEACHER

1. Tony's cousin gave him the nickname "Can't Get Right." Has someone's offhand comment ever become a label you had to fight against?
2. The gang offered protection, but it came with a cost. What trade-offs have you made for belonging or safety?
3. Tony describes the moment Pops tore up his probation paperwork. What's a moment when someone fought for you harder than you expected?
4. Moving to Plano West changed Tony's trajectory. What opportunity shifted the direction of your life?

ROUND 4: FINDING MY CORNER

1. Tony describes being the new Black kid in a predominantly white school but refusing to let that define him. How do you navigate being the "outsider"?
2. Becoming Class President seemed impossible, but Tony ran anyway. What's something you pursued despite everyone doubting you?
3. Tony credits his social IQ for much of his success. How do you cultivate connection with people who are different from you?
4. The Master of Ceremonies speech at graduation was a turning point. What public moment forced you to step into a larger version of yourself?

Part II: Fight Night

ROUND 5: BLOOD, SWEAT AND SCORECARDS

1. Tony started boxing at twenty, far older than most professionals. What's something you started "late" that ended up being exactly on time?
2. He describes the moment he fell in love with the sport. What activity or pursuit has captured you the same way?
3. Tony talks about showing up to the gym even when exhausted. What does 110% commitment look like in your life right now?
4. The first loss taught Tony more than wins. What failure has taught you the most?

ROUND 6: BETWEEN THE ROPES

1. Tony learned there's a difference between knowing how to do something and understanding why. Where do you need to move from mechanics to strategy?
2. He describes adapting his learning style when his coach couldn't reach him. When have you had to find a different teacher to master something?
3. The Golden Gloves wins changed his identity. What achievement shifted how you saw yourself?
4. Tony writes about the loneliness of the grind. How do you sustain motivation when no one is watching?

ROUND 7: CHANGING CORNERS

1. Tony had to leave coaches that helped him grow in order to reach the next level. When have you had to move on from something good to reach something better?
2. Derrick James adapted his training style to reach Tony. What does it look like to mentor someone who doesn't learn the way you do?
3. The path to the Olympics required sacrifice in every area of life. What have you sacrificed in pursuit of a goal?
4. Tony describes fighting opponents with more experience and still believing he could win. Where does your confidence come from when you're outmatched?

ROUND 8: FIGHT TO FINISH

1. The detached retina ended Tony's career without warning. How do you cope with endings you didn't choose?
2. Tony could have been bitter, but he chose gratitude. How do you practice gratitude in the face of disappointment?
3. He writes that boxing didn't just build his career; it saved his life. What pursuit or discipline has done the same for you?
4. The transition from fighter to trainer wasn't immediate or easy. What bridges have you had to build between one chapter and the next?

Part III: After The Bell

ROUND 9: THE PIVOT

1. Tony's business success came from skills he didn't know he was building while boxing. What skills are you developing now that might serve a different purpose later?
2. He writes about "guilt of success" and feeling bad for outgrowing people. Have you experienced this? How did you navigate it?
3. Nate became a mentor in life and business. Who plays that role for you? Are you playing it for someone else?
4. The pivot wasn't a single moment but a series of choices. What small choices are shaping your next chapter?

ROUND 10: THE PLAYBOOK

1. Tony talks about building his own table when he wasn't given a seat. What tables are you building instead of waiting for an invitation?
2. He credits much of his success to relationships. How intentional are you about investing in the people around you?
3. The chapter addresses failure as part of the process. What's your relationship with failure right now?
4. Tony's wife Ashley is described as his "peace." Who or what grounds you?

ROUND 11: THE STABLE

1. TMACK Elite trains champions, but also changes lives. What's the difference between building a business and building a legacy?
2. Tony writes about including the outsider. How do you create space for people who don't "fit"?
3. The chapter emphasizes the power of women in Tony's life. Who are the women who shaped you?
4. Tony describes "The Four Pillars of People." Who are your pillars?

ROUND 12: WATCHING THE FILM

1. Athletes watch game film to improve. How do you review your own "footage", your decisions, patterns, and habits?
2. Tony writes about the danger of complacency after success. Where are you at risk of coasting?
3. Giving and forgiving are linked for Tony. Where do you need to give more freely? Where do you need to forgive?
4. The book ends with gratitude and readiness for the next round. What's your next round?

FINAL REFLECTION QUESTIONS

1. Which "Round" in this book hit hardest for you? Why?
2. What's one lesson from Tony's story you want to apply immediately?
3. Tony rewrote this book because the first version wasn't ready, and neither was he. What in your life needs to be "rewritten" with the wisdom you have now?
4. Who do you need to share this book with?

GROUP EXERCISE: CORNER QUESTIONS

Select 3-5 Corner Questions from throughout the book. Have each group member answer one aloud. Discuss how the answers differ based on individual experiences.

FOR COACHES, MENTORS, AND TEAM LEADERS

1. How can you adapt your teaching style to reach someone who learns differently?
2. What systems in your program might be limiting potential instead of unlocking it?
3. How do you balance accountability with compassion?
4. What does it mean to build a "stable" versus just a team?

"The bell just rang. On to the next round."

www.ingramcontent.com/pod-product-compliance
Lightning Source LLC
LaVergne TN
LVHW101321110826
845152LV00011B/27

9781961781832